Cooking for Two

The Cookbook Library

 Flame Tree has been creating **family-friendly**, **classic** and **beginner recipes** for our best-selling cookbooks for over ten years now. Our mission is to offer you a wide range of **expert-tested** dishes, while providing **straightforward** step-by-step photos and clear images of the final dish so that you can match it to your own results. Further information is available at **FlameTreeRecipes.com**

Publisher & Creative Director: Nick Wells
Senior Project Editor: Catherine Taylor
Art Director: Mike Spender
Digital Design & Production: Chris Herbert

This is a **FLAME TREE** Book

FLAME TREE PUBLISHING

Crabtree Hall, Crabtree Lane
Fulham, London SW6 6TY
United Kingdom
www.flametreepublishing.com

Flame Tree is part of Flame Tree Publishing Ltd

First published 2010
Copyright © 2010 Flame Tree Publishing

13 14
5 7 9 10 8 6

ISBN: 978-1-84786-697-4

Printed in Singapore

All images © Flame Tree Publishing Ltd, except the below.
Courtesy of Shutterstock and © the following photographers: 14, 42r Elena Elisseeva; 15 Yuri Arcurs; 16 Pakhnyushcha; 17 Monkey Business Images;
18 Sakala; 19 Alan Gordine; 20 Ashley Whitworth; 21 Christopher Elwell; 22b LouLouPhotos; 22t omers; 23b Anyka; 23t Gala_Kan; 24 Maksim Shmeljov;
25 sbarabu; 27 Gilmanshin; 28t Payless Images; 28b Viktorus; 29 Tyler Olson; 30 MikLav; 31 PHB.cz (Richard Semik); 32 Justin Paget; 33t 3445128471;
34 Joe Gough; 37b fotogiunta; 37t Robyn Mackenzie; 38 Zamula Artem; 39 Andi Berger; 40t Eugene Berman; 40b SergioZ; 42l ason

Cooking for Two

Quick and Easy, Proven Recipes

FLAME TREE
PUBLISHING

Contents

Soups, Starters & Lighter Dishes

Few of us cook three- or even two-course meals – especially after we get home from work during the week, as we simply don't have the time and energy. However, this section contains a great selection of dishes that could work as lunches for the weekend or made ahead for the week, or as starters for that occasional more ambitious meal.

Fish & Seafood 88

Fish can be a healthy and quick dinner option. It is easy to cook for two as you can often buy two whole fish and have one each, or steaks and fillets often come packed in twos. In this section a mouthwatering selection of seafood dishes are suggested, from a simple, fresh and zingy Seared Salmon & Lemon Linguine to a warming Tuna & Mushroom Ragout.

Meat & Poultry 122

You may not be able to do a whole Sunday roast without wondering how to use the rest of the chicken, but there are plenty of meaty dishes you can whip up in no time at all, without wasting any meat (just make sure you read about how best to store all that mince you got on special offer – *see* pages 20–31). From classic Spaghetti Bolognese to a lip-smacking Aromatic Chicken Curry, there is much to tempt you here.

Vegetables..174

Whether you are vegetarian or simply watching your meat intake, there is much to inspire in this section. Everyone likes a stir-fry, or why not try the Mediterranean-infused Pasta with Courgettes, Rosemary & Lemon? Either way you'll have supper on the table in no time. Don't be afraid to try making your own pizza – share one or have one each – and nothing beats the divine sweet and salty flavours of Chargrilled Vegetable & Goats' Cheese Pizza.

Special Occasions...210

Whether you want to cook up something a little more interesting for a romantic evening, have something to celebrate or simply feel like flexing your culinary muscles, why not give one of these recipes a go? They may have a slightly more 'luxury' ingredient or possess that extra flourish, but it'll be worth it – from the deeply satisfying Scallop & Potato Gratin to the special Pheasant with Sage & Blueberries.

Cooking Ahead 244

This section concentrates on cooking and freezing your home-cooked meals. A freezer full with your delicious meals is such a bonus when time is precious and it is so easy to do. So, when looking for something to cook for supper, get ahead and make double the amount, then freeze half – perfect. Just because you are cooking for two does not mean you cannot cook those classics such as lasagne or quiche – and you don't have to eat them all at once!

One-off supper suggestion: Brandied Lamb Chops, page 140

One-off supper suggestion: Chargrilled Vegetable & Goats' Cheese Pizza, page 193

Desserts & Cakes 280

Here we provide a selection of delicious desserts that can be made for just two people, along with a few suggestions of tarts and cakes that you can either keep for quite some time in an airtight container (ideal for a treat with a cup of tea in the evening) or freeze in portions for a more interesting dessert. Tantalise your taste buds with a refined Crème Brûlée with Sugared Raspberries or a moreish Luxury Carrot Cake.

Introduction

Who Cooks for Two?

It is not just newlyweds or partners who cook for two – there are the parents who have experienced the joys and tribulations of bringing up their families and are now, for the first time in perhaps twenty years, on their own as the kids have left home and no longer need Mum to cook for them. Relearning how to cut down quantities is not easy after what seems a lifetime of cooking for more, and here there is a grave danger of massive overcooking and even wastage. There are also of course single parents who are cooking for themselves and a teenager perhaps; and then there are the flatmates who often share the cooking.

The problem is: how to reduce a favourite recipe, or an appealing recipe you have discovered, in order to serve fewer people but still retain its delicious flavour and nutritional content?

The Difficulties of Cooking for Two

Arguably, it is easier to cook for four, or even eight, people than for two. It is far easier to double up a recipe than to cut it in half. Even if you're a dab hand with the calculator, it's not always as straightforward as simply chopping each amount in half.

Many recipes do not easily break down into smaller quantities – especially the amount of liquid required, for instance; and have you ever tried splitting an egg yolk in two?

When cooking smaller amounts, there is also the danger of wasting food and money by cooking too much and not knowing what to do with the leftovers. You may attempt to save food for another time but then run the risk of spoilage or food poisoning if the food is not stored correctly or reheated sufficiently. This cookbook answers those basic needs with tips on how to save money by buying in bulk without wastage, then cooking and freezing both fresh and cooked foods.

Once you have absorbed the invaluable information in the first part of this book, take your pick from a range of delicious recipes that have all been tailored to serve two people or that are perfect for cooking in bulk – cooking ahead so that you can just reach into the freezer for a tasty home-made meal.

Why not use this opportunity to reap the benefits of cooking together, whether it is quality time with a friend or loved one or a chance to impart cooking knowledge to your teenager? *Cooking for Two* will show you that there is no need to rely on ready meals, takeaways and dinner out – it is easy to prepare a healthy, nutritious meal for two without spending a fortune and without wastage.

Shopping for Two

As we know, food has become more expensive so it is even more important that ingredients are not wasted – this is essentially true with everyone. There are two ways of shopping – the expensive way or the sensible way.

You can simply go out and wander around food shops, supermarkets and farmers' markets with no plan or idea of the food you need, simply buying at random, picking up whatever takes your fancy, then arriving home with a variety of ingredients and absolutely no idea what you are going to do with them. Often the ingredients are shoved in the cupboard or refrigerator, then forgotten and end up being discarded. This is, unsurprisingly, the most expensive way of shopping.

Planning is Key

You can do that, or you can plan. Plan your menu for the week and then make a list of what ingredients you need in order to cook the chosen recipes. This way, you will save money, save ingredients and most of all save yourself from unnecessary anxiety and stress. So first, decide together what meals you are going to cook. If you are not that experienced in cooking, do not be too adventurous; keep it simple, looking at meals that perhaps use only a few ingredients and are quick to prepare and cook. Have a look in your store cupboard to see what ingredients you already have, then look at the recipe and write a list. When shopping from a list, be strict with yourself and try not to deviate – only buy food that you know you will use.

Special Offers and Bulk Buying

It can still be a good idea to be aware of all the special offers that are on display, but remember that this is yet another way that money can be spent and wasted. Often you can end up buying food because it looks a good bargain only to discover that is not – perhaps the use-by date is about to expire, or if the offer is a 'BOGOF' (buy one get one free), this can lead to thoughts of 'I've got loads of this so I can use more', resulting in the 'free' food being used far more quickly than if you had only bought the one item, or, indeed, over-consumption.

When cooking for two, sometimes it is difficult to buy in small quantities, especially if you do not have any food stores or markets that sell fresh unpacked foods, so 'bulk' buying may be unavoidable. This need not be a problem, as long as you are aware that you will need to use the food before its expiry date or store it cleverly. So, for instance, if the butcher has a special offer on stewing meat, it might be a good buy, but only if not left in the refrigerator – either cook it all and freeze in suitable portions, or freeze the raw meat in useable amounts – do not freeze one big lump of meat that can then only be split up once defrosted (you cannot re-freeze defrosted food).

Store Cupboard Items

An essential part of any kitchen is the store cupboard. Here all manner of foods are stored for use in all kinds of dishes – many will be canned, bottled or dried. These items will generally keep for a long while, in some cases indefinitely, and so are great for those who are cooking for two and thus cannot use up ingredients very quickly.

What to Buy

So what should you buy if starting from scratch for your store cupboard and freezer? Obviously this will depend on your personal likes and dislikes, however there are some basic ingredients that are always a good idea to have at hand no matter what you will be cooking. All of these will keep well.

Spices Buy whole black peppercorns and keep them in a pepper mill so that the pepper can be ground fresh each time. Some people like to have salt, so keep some sea salt, again in a mill so that it can be freshly ground. Coriander, cumin, cinnamon, mixed spice, curry powder (you can always buy other spices to make your own curry powder as you become more experienced), chilli powder, turmeric or saffron and vanilla extract are all good to have.

Dried Goods These should include plain white or wholemeal flour for thickening sauces, sugar for sweetening and dried fruits which work well when a few are added to savoury dishes.

Pulses and Beans These could include split red and green lentils, canned mixed beans as well as dried or canned red kidney beans and of course baked beans for the quick healthy snack (if the reduced salt and sugar version!).

Rice, Noodles and Pasta The essential rice to have is white or brown long grain, for everyday, then basmati, for curries, and jasmine to accompany stir-fries. Egg or cellophane (stir-fry) noodles are useful to have. Plus of course some pasta such as spaghetti and pasta shapes.

How to Keep Store Cupboard Items

These items may last indefinitely, but they still need care in order to keep them at their best. First of all, the cupboard needs to be dark and dry. This will ensure that ingredients stay in good condition for as long as possible after opening. Some will need storing in the refrigerator after opening. There are a few other points to remember when buying specific store cupboard ingredients.

Canned Foods When buying, check that there are no dents in the can and that it is perfectly dry. Once opened, if not using all of the contents, empty the remainder into a small bowl, cover with clingfilm and store for no more than 2–3 days in the refrigerator.

Spices These must only be kept in the dark and bought frequently. The light and heat will quickly destroy their pungency and flavour and this also applies once opened. Spices such as cumin, cinnamon and coriander are in fact better bought as seeds and then ground as required. This gives the maximum flavour and stops the spices from tasting 'musty'.

Sauces Many sauces, such as soy sauce, tomato ketchup, Worcestershire and Tabasco, will keep indefinitely in a dark cupboard, but some will need to be kept in the refrigerator once opened. This applies to sauces such as tartar, horseradish, mayonnaise and salad cream. Check the bottles to see what the manufacturer recommends and look at the use-by dates.

Dried Foods Foods such as ready-to-eat dried apricots, sultanas, raisins and nuts, including ground almonds, will keep very well in a dark cupboard. Once opened, place in screw-top glass jars or airtight plastic containers. This also applies to flour, sugars, cereals and pulses.

Oils and Vinegars Vinegar will keep almost indefinitely in a cool dark cupboard, as will all oils. Do not keep olive oil, especially extra-virgin and specially flavoured olive oil, in the refrigerator as it will quickly become cloudy and the very delicate flavour of the oil will be destroyed.

Storing & Cooking Advice

So you have planned your meals for the week and you've successfully bought everything you need. Now comes the task of giving all the produce the best possible chance of lasting until needed, cooking your meals and storing any accidental or deliberate leftovers.

The Larder

Store cupboard foods should be kept in the larder, the old-fashioned name for a large dry cupboard where food can be kept. This enables the kitchen area to be kept clean and tidy, thus making cooking far easier for it is difficult to obtain good results if working in a messy, untidy place. We have already learnt about store cupboard items but here are some reminders:

Cans All canned foods can be kept in the larder. Remember that once a can is opened, any leftovers must be placed in a small dish or bowl, covered and stored in the refrigerator.

Jars Most jars of food are fine if kept unopened in the larder but check once opened whether they should be kept in the refrigerator.

Dried Food Flour, pulses, rice, pasta, sugar, fruit and nuts are best, once the packet is opened, if stored in a screw-top or Kilner glass jar and this will help maintain the freshness of the product.

Spices These can be kept in the larder in the jars they are purchased in. Do not be tempted to display on a work surface as the light destroys their flavour.

Be Organised It is advisable to keep the different categories of food together so that it is easier to see at a glance what you have and what needs to be replaced.

The Refrigerator

It is vital that food is stored correctly and that hygiene is strictly observed with all foods so as to keep fit and healthy and avoid stomach upsets. A vital element of food safety is how and where food is stored. This applies to all foods, fresh, frozen, canned and dried. How is this achieved?

Most fresh food should be kept in the refrigerator at a temperature of 5°C/41°F, so a thermometer is a good investment to ensure that the refrigerator is functioning correctly. When the weather is very hot, turn the temperature setting to 3 or 4°C while the heat continues.

Foods to be stored in the refrigerator can be kept in their original wrappers, provided the wrappers are sealed. Once opened, the food should be wrapped in nonstick baking or greaseproof paper and, if liked, a polythene bag as well to prevent the food from drying out.

Meat and Fish

Both uncooked and cooked meat and fish should be kept in the refrigerator but, depending on how quickly you are going to use the product, you may find it advisable to freeze some. Use fresh and cooked meat within 2–3 days of purchase, and fish within 24 hours.

If to be consumed immediately, fresh meats and fish should be removed from their original wrappings, placed on a plate and lightly covered with nonstick baking or greaseproof paper and placed towards the bottom of the refrigerator so that their juices cannot drip onto other foods and spread contamination. Keep cooked meats towards the centre of the refrigerator.

Dairy Products

All dairy products, including yogurts, cheese, butter, milk, cream, crème fraîche and fromage frais, need refrigerating. They will keep in the refrigerator quite happily for 1–2 weeks providing that the use-by date has not expired and the refrigerator is at the correct temperature.

Cheese can be kept towards the centre of the refrigerator while yogurts, cream, cheese, butter and spreads towards the top.

Fruit and Vegetables

Fresh fruit and veg are different. They both need to be eaten as soon as possible and it is a good idea not to buy in bulk, but to buy little and often, otherwise there is the danger that both will be past their prime and their vitamins and minerals will be minimal. With that in mind, try buying locally grown produce rather than produce grown hundreds of miles away.

Salad and vegetables should be placed in the salad trays in the refrigerator, used as quickly as possible and washed as required. It is also advisable to wash the pre-packed salad leaves that are now so readily available even though they are sold as pre-washed.

Root vegetables such as carrots, turnips and parsnips, as well as onions and garlic, are fine if left in a cool dry place. Potatoes are best stored in brown paper bags or cloth bags that are sold by kitchen shops, not in the polythene bags they are normally bought in, as this will quickly turn the potatoes green or slimy. Potatoes that have turned green should not be eaten.

Eggs

Eggs are normally stamped with a use-by date and are best kept in the refrigerator for up to three weeks. Place the eggs in the egg trays located in the door, often above the milk and juice. They should never be frozen in their shells, however egg whites can be frozen for up to one year. Thaw in the refrigerator and use as soon as they thaw. Yolks do not freeze well.

Sauces

Some sauces recommend that once open they too should be stored in the refrigerator. These can be placed towards the top. Take care to use within the time recommended on the jar once opened.

Cooked Foods and Dishes

Cooked ham, bacon, smoked salmon and pâté, and dishes using cooked meat and fish, such as lasagne, fish and meat pies and stews, as well as cooked fruit, pies, crumbles, trifle and mousses, should also be kept lightly covered in the refrigerator. Place on the middle to top shelves.

The Freezer

Many ingredients, such as poultry, fish, meat, fruit and vegetables, as well as dairy and bakery products, can be frozen. As with the refrigerator, however, there are certain rules for storing food in the freezer. It is vital that the food is stored at the correct temperature of -5˚C/23˚F and for the correct period of time. Food does not stay the same for ever and after a certain period of time it will deteriorate both in flavour and texture even in the freezer – this will vary according to the food.

If you have a separate freezer with a freezing compartment, switch the freezer to rapid-freeze for six hours before freezing any fresh food. Leave until completely frozen, then remove and place in the main body of the freezer. Remember to return the freezer to its normal setting. If you do not have a separate freezing compartment (this will probably be a fridge-freezer), place the food in the freezer tray (normally located at the top of the fridge), press the freezer button and freeze for 24 hours. Remember to switch off the freezer button. In any case, refer to the manufacturer's instructions.

Meat and Poultry

Meat and poultry should only be frozen if not previously frozen – check what you are buying. Either cook the meat or poultry first and freeze, or freeze raw. Divide into portions, then wrap in nonstick baking or greaseproof paper, label and date, then place in freezer bags. Leave in the rapid-freeze compartment until solid. Remove and store in the main body of the freezer.

Seafood and Shellfish

Most fresh (unfrozen) fish in the shops has not been frozen before, but always check first – as we know, no foods should be refrozen if previously frozen (unless they have been cooked thoroughly first before being refrozen). Watch out with shellfish, though, as often this has already been frozen and thawed to sell – great care should be taken in order to avoid stomach upsets. Wrap and store as for meat and remember, if using previously frozen seafood, prepare and cook the recipe, then place the portion to be frozen into a freezeable container, label and date, then freeze as above. When reheating, ensure that the dish is thoroughly thawed before reheating and that it is piping hot before serving.

Open Freezing

In order to freeze, say, individual pastries, berries, vegetables or other foods not in a sauce, without them all sticking together in one big lump, so that you can take what you need from the freezer without having to thaw a whole batch, you can open freeze them. Spread out on a baking sheet or a tray so that no items are touching each other and place in the freezer uncovered until completely frozen. Then pack either in freezer bags or containers.

Essential Points and Top Tips

Here is a re-cap of the essential points to remember when buying food for the freezer:

- Set the freezer to rapid-freeze for the manufacturer's recommended time and remember to return the freezer to its normal setting once the food is frozen.

- Buy food as fresh as possible ensuring it has not passed its sell-by date.

- Divide into the quantities you require as soon as possible after purchase, then wrap, label, date and freeze.

- Use freezer wrap or nonstick baking or greaseproof paper with freezer bags to wrap the foods and then label clearly with both date and what kind of food you are freezing. It is often a good idea to label both inside the bag as well as on the outside, as often the label on the outside will fall off.

- If freezing food you have cooked yourself, plastic freezeable containers with lids are a good idea. Allow the food to cool as quickly as possible (but do not put in the refrigerator to cool), then place the food in suitably-sized containers, seal with the lid, label and date, then place in the rapid-freeze compartment and freeze.

- Make sure that you rotate the food in the freezer, placing the food already frozen at the top and the food that has just been added at the bottom.

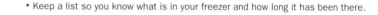

- Keep a list so you know what is in your freezer and how long it has been there.

- Never re-freeze food that has been previously frozen unless it has been cooked first, and always ensure that the food is thoroughly thawed unless it is a commercially frozen product and the packaging gives instructions for the food to be cooked from frozen.

- Cover the food to be thawed lightly and place on a plate or in a dish and thaw in the refrigerator.

In an Emergency

For example, if there is a power cut, do not open the door. If possible cover the freezer with a blanket ensuring that the pipes and condenser are not covered. The food should keep frozen for up to 30 hours. In the event of all the food thawing, cook the meat and fish as soon as possible and then it is possible to refreeze this cooked food. Other food should be consumed within 24 hours and then any left must be thrown away.

Freezer Storage Times

White fish	6–8 months
Oily fish	3–4 months
Beef, lamb and pork	4–6 months
Poultry and game	4–6 months
Offal	3–4 months
Bacon and ham joints	3–4 months
Sliced bacon, cured meats, fresh mince and sausages	2–3 months
Soups and sauces	3 months
Stock	6 months
Prepared meals	4–6 months
Cakes	4–6 months
Bread	2–3 months
Ice cream	3–4 months
Hard cheese	4–6 months
Soft cheese	3–4 months
Blanched vegetables	10–12 months
Un-blanched vegetables	3–4 weeks
Commercially frozen vegetables	up to 1 year
Fruit juice	4–6 months
Open-frozen fruit	(*see* page 26) 6–8 months
Fruit and vegetable purée	6–8 months

Cooking For Two Made Easy

You are now ready to start cooking, but you are not sure how to start, as all the other cookbooks' recipes you have looked at are for larger servings and it is confusing trying to cut the recipe for two people. It is particularly frustrating if this is your first attempt to cook for someone else – it is daunting enough, and you cannot afford to waste either the time or the money you have spent. Help is at hand.

Follow Procedure

Before you start cooking make sure you are happy with your chosen recipe. Then follow these steps and everything should go smoothly.

- Most importantly, read the recipe from start to finish – this will ensure that there are no instructions you are not sure about or that come as a surprise.

- Assemble all the ingredients and the equipment you need. This includes chopping boards, knives, measuring spoons, bowls and the necessary pans. Reading the recipe will enable you to do this.

- Check if the recipe uses cooked or prepared food such as cooked rice, fresh breadcrumbs, hard-boiled eggs or chopped herbs – if so do these first.

- Preheat the oven if necessary.

- Begin cooking. Take time to check that each step is completed before you move on to the next step.

- Invest in a timer and oven thermometer – this way you can ensure that you cook the food correctly both in time and temperature. It is important to bear in mind that ovens can vary enormously both in temperature and performance. So if your timings seem to vary considerably or the food is not cooking as it should, get your oven checked by either the manufacturer or a technician.

Cooking Ahead

If you have bought too much for one meal, either by accident or design, then this the ideal time to cook and freeze. Choose your recipes, ensuring that you have sufficient amounts of all the required ingredients. Then cook and allow to cool as quickly as possible, without refrigerating. A good way to do this is to stand the dish of food in a large bowl of cold water.

If there are only two of you, it is important to divide the food into the size of portions you require (as you are not going to eat a whole pie between you for instance, and remember – you cannot refreeze it once it is defrosted), place in containers, cover with the lids, label, date and freeze. The following dishes are ideal for cooking and freezing:

Casseroles and Stews Such as goulash, sweet-and-sour pork, coq au vin, curries and hot pot.

Pies Shepherd's pie, fish pie, steak and kidney and chicken, as well as fruit pies, crumbles and lemon meringue pie.

Dishes Using Mince These include chilli con carne, lasagne, cannelloni, bolgnese sauce and meat loaf.

Pastries Both sweet and savoury.

Cakes It is possible to freeze cakes but, as they generally have a reasonably long shelf life, it really is not necessary and can dry the cake out too much.

Desserts Cream desserts will also freeze well, but milk desserts do not.

Cooking With this Book

You will see more hints and tips alongside the recipes in this book, which will enable you to cook with confidence, using fresh ingredients, safe in the knowledge that you will easily be able to buy and cook in bulk if you wish and then freeze any leftovers for use on another day, or just cook a meal for two people at one sitting, with no wastage or excessive expense.

So get your partner and let the fun begin. Happy cooking for two!

Hygiene in the Kitchen

This section provides you with a useful reminder for essential kitchen hygiene – however many people you are cooking for! It is well worth remembering that many foods can carry some form of bacteria. In most cases, the worst it will lead to is a bout of food poisoning or gastroenteritis, although for certain groups this can be more serious. The risk can be reduced or eliminated by good food hygiene and proper cooking.

Do not buy food that is past its sell-by date and do not consume any food that is past its use-by date. When buying food, use the eyes and nose. If the food looks tired, limp or a bad colour or it has a rank, acrid or simply bad smell, do not buy or eat it under any circumstances.

Regularly clean, defrost and clear out the refrigerator or freezer – it is worth checking the packaging to see exactly how long each product is safe to freeze.

Dish cloths and tea towels must be washed and changed regularly. Ideally use disposable cloths which should be replaced on a daily basis. More durable cloths should be left to soak in bleach, then washed in the washing machine on a boil wash.

Always keep your hands, cooking utensils and food preparation surfaces clean and never allow pets to climb on to any work surfaces.

Buying

As we have seen, avoid massive bulk buying where possible, especially fresh produce such as meat, poultry, fish, fruit and vegetables – unless buying for the freezer. Fresh foods lose their nutritional value rapidly, so buying a little at a time minimises loss of nutrients. It also eliminates a packed refrigerator (which reduces the effectiveness of the refrigeration process). When buying frozen foods, ensure that they are not heavily iced on the outside. Place in the freezer as soon as possible after purchase.

Preparation

Make sure that all work surfaces and utensils are clean and dry. Separate chopping boards should be used for raw and cooked meats, fish and vegetables. It is worth washing all fruit and vegetables regardless of whether they are going to be eaten raw or lightly cooked. Do not reheat food more than once.

All poultry must be thoroughly thawed before cooking. Leave the food in the refrigerator until it is completely thawed. Once defrosted, the chicken should be cooked as soon as possible. Again, the only time food can be refrozen is when the food has been thoroughly thawed, then cooked.

All poultry and game (except for duck) must be cooked thoroughly. When cooked, the juices will run clear (pierce with a knife or skewer to test).

Other meats, such as minced meat and pork, should be cooked right the way through.

Fish should turn opaque, be firm in texture and break easily into large flakes.

Storing, Refrigerating and Freezing

Meat, poultry, fish, seafood and dairy products should all be refrigerated. The temperature of the refrigerator should be between 1–5°C/34–41°F while the freezer temperature should not rise above -18°C/-0.4°F. When refrigerating cooked food, allow it to cool down completely before refrigerating. Hot food will raise the temperature of the refrigerator and possibly affect or spoil other food stored in it.

Food within the refrigerator and freezer should always be covered. Raw and cooked food should be stored in separate parts of the refrigerator. Cooked food should be kept on the top shelves of the refrigerator, while raw meat, poultry and fish should be placed on bottom shelves to avoid drips and cross-contamination.

High-Risk Foods

Certain foods may carry risks to people who are considered vulnerable such as the elderly, the ill, pregnant women, babies and those suffering from a recurring illness. It is advisable to avoid those foods which belong to a higher-risk category.

Eggs

There is a slight chance that some eggs carry the bacteria salmonella. Cook the eggs until both the yolk and the white are firm to eliminate this risk. Sauces including Hollandaise, mayonnaise, mousses, soufflés and meringues all use raw or lightly cooked eggs, as do custard-based dishes, ice creams and sorbets. These are all considered high-risk foods to the vulnerable groups mentioned above.

Meat and Poultry

Certain meats and poultry also carry the potential risk of salmonella and so should be cooked thoroughly until the juices run clear and there is no pinkness left.

Unpasteurised Products

Unpasteurised products such as milk, cheese (especially soft cheese), pâté, meat (both raw and cooked) all have the potential risk of listeria and should be avoided.

Seafood

When buying seafood, buy from a reputable source. Fish should have bright clear eyes, shiny skin and bright pink or red gills. The fish should feel stiff to the touch, with a slight smell of sea air and iodine. The flesh of fish steaks and fillets should be translucent with no signs of discolouration.

Avoid any molluscs that are open or do not close when tapped lightly. Univalves such as cockles or winkles should withdraw into their shells when lightly prodded. Squid and octopus should have firm flesh and a pleasant sea smell.

Nutrition

A healthy and well-balanced diet is the body's primary energy source. In children, it constitutes the building blocks for future health as well as providing lots of energy. In adults, it encourages self-healing and regeneration within the body. A well-balanced diet will provide the body with all the essential nutrients it needs. This can be achieved by eating a variety of foods, demonstrated in the pyramid shown here.

Fats

Fats fall into two categories: saturated and unsaturated fats. It is very important that a healthy balance is achieved within the diet. Fats are an essential part of the diet and a source of energy and provide essential fatty acids and fat soluble vitamins. The right balance of fats should boost the body's immunity to infection and keep muscles, nerves and arteries in good condition.

Saturated Fats

Saturated fats are of animal origin and are hard when stored at room temperature. They can be found in dairy produce, meat, eggs, margarines and hard white cooking fat (lard) as well as in manufactured products such as pies, biscuits and cakes. A high intake of saturated fat over many years has been proven to increase heart

Fats
milk, yoghurt,
cheese and oils

Proteins
meat, fish, poultry, eggs,
nuts and pulses

Fruit and Vegetables

Starchy Carbohydrates
cereals, potatoes, bread, rice and pasta

disease and high blood cholesterol levels and often leads to weight gain. The aim of a healthy diet is to keep the fat content low in the foods that we eat. Lowering the amount of saturated fat that we consume is very important, but this does not mean that it is good to consume lots of other types of fat.

Unsaturated Fats

There are two kinds of unsaturated fats: poly-unsaturated fats and monounsaturated fats. Poly-unsaturated fats include the following oils: safflower oil, soybean oil, corn oil and sesame oil. Within the poly-unsaturated group are Omega oils. The Omega-3 oils are of significant interest because they have been found to be particularly beneficial to coronary health and can encourage brain growth and development. Omega-3 oils are mainly derived from oily fish such as salmon, mackerel, herring, pilchards and sardines. It is recommended that we should eat these types of fish

at least once a week. However, for those who do not eat fish or who are vegetarians, liver oil supplements are available in most supermarkets and health shops. It is suggested that these supplements should be taken on a daily basis.

The most popular oils that are high in monounsaturates are olive oil, sunflower oil and peanut oil. The Mediterranean diet, which is based on a diet high in monounsaturated fats, is recommended for heart health. Also, monounsaturated fats are known to help reduce the levels of LDL (the bad) cholestrol.

Proteins

Composed of amino acids (proteins' building bricks), proteins perform a wide variety of essential functions for the body including supplying energy and building and repairing tissues. Good sources of proteins are eggs, milk, yoghurt, cheese, meat, fish, poultry, eggs, nuts and pulses. (See the second level of the pyramid.) Some of these foods, however, contain saturated fats. To strike a nutritional balance eat generous amounts of vegetable protein foods such as soya, beans, lentils, peas and nuts.

Fruit and Vegetables

Not only are fruit and vegetables the most visually appealing foods, but they are extremely good for us, providing essential vitamins and minerals essential for growth, repair and protection in the human body. Fruit and vegetables are low in calories and are responsible for regulating the body's metabolic processes and controlling the composition of its fluids and cells.

Minerals

Calcium Important for healthy bones and teeth, nerve transmission, muscle contraction, blood clotting and hormone function. Calcium promotes a healthy heart, improves skin, relieves aching muscles and bones, maintains the correct acid-alkaline balance and reduces menstrual cramps. Good sources are dairy products, small bones of small fish, nuts, pulses, fortified white flours, breads and green leafy vegetables.

Chromium Part of the glucose tolerance factor, chromium balances blood sugar levels, helps to normalise hunger and reduce cravings, improves lifespan, helps protect DNA and is essential for heart function. Good sources are brewer's yeast, wholemeal bread, rye bread, oysters, potatoes, green peppers, butter and parsnips.

Iodine Important for the manufacture of thyroid hormones and for normal development. Good sources of iodine are seafood, seaweed, milk and dairy products.

Iron As a component of haemoglobin, iron carries oxygen around the body. It is vital for normal growth and development. Good sources are liver, corned beef, red meat, fortified breakfast cereals, pulses, green leafy vegetables, egg yolk and cocoa and cocoa products.

Magnesium Important for efficient functioning of metabolic enzymes and development of the skeleton. Magnesium promotes healthy muscles by helping them to relax and is therefore good for PMS. It is also important for heart muscles and the nervous system. Good sources are nuts, green vegetables, meat, cereals, milk and yoghurt.

Phosphorus Forms and maintains bones and teeth, builds muscle tissue, helps maintain the body's pH and aids metabolism and energy production. Phosphorus is present in almost all foods.

Potassium Enables nutrients to move into cells, while waste products move out; promotes healthy nerves and muscles; maintains fluid balance in the body; helps secretion of insulin for blood sugar control to produce constant energy; relaxes muscles; maintains heart functioning and stimulates gut movement to encourage proper elimination. Good sources are fruit, vegetables, milk and bread.

Selenium Antioxidant properties help to protect against free radicals and carcinogens. Selenium reduces inflammation, stimulates the immune system to fight infections, promotes a healthy heart and helps vitamin E's action. It is also required for the male reproductive system and is needed for metabolism. Good sources are tuna, liver, kidney, meat, eggs, cereals, nuts and dairy products.

Sodium Important in helping to control body fluid and balance, preventing dehydration. Sodium is involved in muscle and nerve function and helps move nutrients into cells. All foods are good sources, however processed, pickled and salted foods are richest in sodium.

Zinc Important for metabolism and the healing of wounds. It also aids ability to cope with stress, promotes a healthy nervous system and brain especially in the growing foetus, aids bones and teeth formation and is essential for constant energy. Good sources are liver, meat, pulses, whole-grain cereals, nuts and oysters.

Vitamins

Vitamin A Important for cell growth and development and for the formation of visual pigments in the eye. Vitamin A comes in two forms: retinol and beta-carotenes. Retinol is found in liver, meat and meat products and whole milk and its products. Beta-carotene is a powerful antioxidant and is found in red and yellow fruit and vegetables such as carrots, mangoes and apricots.

Vitamin B1 Important in releasing energy from carboydrate-containing foods. Good sources are yeast and yeast products, bread, fortified breakfast cereals and potatoes.

Vitamin B2 Important for metabolism of proteins, fats and carbohydrates to produce energy. Good sources are meat, yeast extracts, fortified breakfast cereals and milk and its products.

Vitamin B3 Required for the metabolism of food into energy production. Good sources are milk and milk products, fortified breakfast cereals, pulses, meat, poultry and eggs.

Vitamin B5 Important for the metabolism of food and energy production. All foods are good sources but especially fortified breakfast cereals, whole-grain bread and dairy products.

Vitamin B6 Important for metabolism of protein and fat. Vitamin B6 may also be involved with the regulation of sex hormones. Good sources are liver, fish, pork, soya beans and peanuts.

Vitamin B12 Important for the production of red blood cells and DNA. It is vital for growth and the nervous system. Good sources are meat, fish, eggs, poultry and milk.

Biotin Important for metabolism of fatty acids. Good sources of biotin are liver, kidney, eggs and nuts. Micro-organisms also manufacture this vitamin in the gut.

Vitamin C Important for healing wounds and the formation of collagen which keeps skin and bones strong. It is an important antioxidant. Good sources are fruit, soft summer fruit and vegetables.

Vitamin D Important for absorption and handling of calcium to help build bone strength. Good sources are oily fish, eggs, whole milk and milk products, margarine and of course sufficient exposure to sunlight, as vitamin D is made in the skin.

Vitamin E Important as an antioxidant vitamin helping to protect cell membranes from damage. Good sources are vegetable oils, margarines, seeds, nuts and green vegetables.

Folic Acid Critical during pregnancy for the development of the brain and nerves. It is always essential for brain and nerve function and is needed for utilising protein and red blood cell formation. Good sources are whole-grain cereals, fortified breakfast cereals, green leafy vegetables, oranges and liver.

Vitamin K Important for controlling blood clotting. Good sources are cauliflower, Brussels sprouts, lettuce, cabbage, beans, broccoli, peas, asparagus, potatoes, corn oil, tomatoes and milk.

Carbohydrates

Carbohydrates are an energy source and come in two forms: starch and sugar carbohydrates. Starch carbohydrates are also known as complex carbohydrates and they include all cereals, potatoes, breads, rice and pasta. (See the fourth level of the pyramid). Eating whole-grain varieties of these foods also provides fibre. Diets high in fibre are believed to be beneficial in helping to prevent bowel cancer and can also keep cholesterol down. High-fibre diets are also good for those concerned about weight gain. Fibre is bulky so fills the stomach, therefore reducing hunger pangs.

Sugar carbohydrates, which are also known as fast-release carbohydrates (because of the quick fix of energy they give to the body), include sugar and sugar-sweetened products such as jams and syrups. Milk provides lactose, which is a milk sugar, and fruit provides fructose, which is a fruit sugar.

Soups, Starters & Lighter Dishes

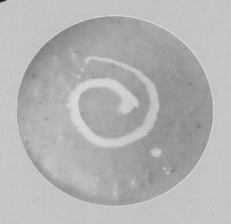

Rice & Tomato Soup

SERVES 2

65 g/2½ oz easy-cook basmati rice
200 g/7 oz canned chopped tomatoes
1 garlic clove, peeled and crushed
grated zest of ½ lime

1 tbsp extra-virgin olive oil
½–1 tsp sugar
salt and freshly ground black pepper
450 ml/¾ pint vegetable stock or water

For the croutons:
1 tbsp ready-made pesto sauce
2 tbsp olive oil
2–3 thin slices ciabatta bread, cut into 1 cm/½ inch cubes

Preheat the oven to 220°C/425°F/Gas Mark 7. Rinse and drain the basmati rice. Place the canned tomatoes with their juice in a large heavy-based saucepan with the garlic, lime zest, oil and sugar. Season to taste with salt and pepper. Bring to the boil, then reduce the heat, cover and simmer for 10 minutes.

Add the boiling vegetable stock or water and the rice, then cook, uncovered, for a further 15–20 minutes, or until the rice is tender. If the soup is too thick, add a little more water. Reserve and keep warm, if the croutons are not ready.

Meanwhile, to make the croutons, mix the pesto and olive oil in a large bowl. Add the bread cubes and toss until they are coated completely with the mixture. Spread on a baking sheet and bake in the preheated oven for 10–15 minutes until golden and crisp, turning them over halfway through cooking. Serve the soup immediately, sprinkled with the warm croutons.

HELPFUL HINT
Store the remaining canned chopped tomatoes in a small glass bowl lightly covered in the refrigerator for up to 3 days.

Tomato & Basil Soup

SERVES 2

450 g/ 1 lb ripe tomatoes, cut in half
2 small garlic cloves
1 tsp olive oil
1 tbsp balsamic vinegar

1 tbsp dark brown sugar
1 tbsp tomato purée
150 ml/¼ pint vegetable stock
3 tbsp natural yogurt
2 tbsp freshly chopped basil

salt and freshly ground black pepper
small basil leaves, to garnish

Preheat the oven to 200°C/400°F/Gas Mark 6. Evenly spread the tomatoes and unpeeled garlic in a single layer in a large roasting tin.

Mix the oil and vinegar together. Drizzle over the tomatoes and sprinkle with the dark brown sugar.

Roast the tomatoes in the preheated oven for 20 minutes until tender and lightly charred in places.

Remove from the oven and allow to cool slightly. When cool enough to handle, squeeze the softened flesh of the garlic from the papery skin. Place with the charred tomatoes in a nylon sieve over a saucepan.

Press the garlic and tomato through the sieve with the back of a wooden spoon.

When all the flesh has been sieved, add the tomato purée and vegetable stock to the pan. Heat gently, stirring occasionally.

HELPFUL HINT

When cooking for just two, take care that you do not add too much seasoning especially salt. Commercial stock normally contains a lot of salt.

In a small bowl, beat the yogurt and basil together and season to taste with salt and pepper. Stir the basil yogurt into the soup. Garnish with basil leaves and serve immediately.

Carrot & Ginger Soup

2 small slices of bread,
    crusts removed
1 tsp yeast extract
2 tsp olive oil
1 small onion, peeled and
    chopped
1 small garlic clove,
    peeled and crushed

½ tsp, or to taste, ground
    ginger
225 g/ 8 oz carrots, peeled
    and chopped
600 ml/ 1 pint vegetable stock
1 cm/½ inch piece root
    ginger, peeled and
    finely grated

salt and freshly ground
    black pepper
1 tbsp lemon juice

To garnish:
chives
strands of lemon zest

Preheat the oven to 180°C/350°F/Gas Mark 4. Roughly chop the bread. Dissolve the yeast extract in 1 tablespoon warm water and mix with the bread.

Spread the bread cubes over a lightly oiled baking tray and bake for 20 minutes, turning halfway through. Remove from the oven and reserve.

Heat the oil in a large saucepan. Gently cook the onion and garlic for 3–4 minutes.

Stir in the ground ginger and cook for 1 minute to release the flavour.

Add the chopped carrots, then stir in the stock and the fresh ginger. Simmer gently for 15–20 minutes.

Remove from the heat and allow to cool a little. Blend until smooth, then season to taste with salt and pepper. Stir in the lemon juice. Garnish with a few bread cubes, the chives and strands of lemon zest and serve immediately with the remaining bread cubes.

HELPFUL HINT

When cooking for two it is a good idea to use smaller saucepans than when cooking for more, as otherwise there is a risk of liquid evaporating quickly and food burning.

Rocket & Potato Soup
with Garlic Croûtons

SERVES 2

350 g/12 oz baby new
  potatoes
600 ml/1 pint chicken or
  vegetable stock
25 g/1 oz rocket leaves
2 slices thick white bread

25 g/1 oz unsalted butter
1 tsp groundnut oil
2 garlic cloves, peeled
  and chopped
50 g/2 oz stale ciabatta
  bread, crusts removed

2 tbsp olive oil
salt and freshly ground
  black pepper
1 tbsp Parmesan cheese,
  finely grated

Scrub the potatoes then cut in half or quarters depending on size. Leave whole if tiny. Place the potatoes in a large saucepan, cover with the stock and simmer gently for 10 minutes. Add the rocket leaves and simmer for a further 5–10 minutes, or until the potatoes are soft and the rocket has wilted.

Meanwhile, make the croutons. Cut the thick, white sliced bread into small cubes and reserve. Heat the butter and groundnut oil in a small frying pan and cook the garlic for 1 minute, stirring well. Remove the garlic. Add the bread cubes to the butter and oil mixture in the frying pan and sauté, stirring continuously, until they are golden brown. Drain the croutons on absorbent kitchen paper and reserve.

Cut the ciabatta bread into small dice and stir into the soup. Cover the saucepan and leave to stand for 10 minutes, or until the bread has absorbed a lot of the liquid.

Stir in the olive oil, season to taste with salt and pepper and serve at once with a few of the garlic croutons scattered over the top and a little grated Parmesan cheese.

Swede, Turnip, Parsnip & Potato Soup

SERVES 2

2 small onions, peeled
25 g/1 oz butter
1 medium carrot, peeled and
  roughly chopped
125 g/4 oz swede, peeled
  and roughly chopped
2 small, about 50 g/2 oz,
  turnips, peeled and

roughly chopped
1 small, about 50 g/2 oz,
  parsnip, peeled and
  roughly chopped
1 small, about 50 g/2 oz,
  potato, peeled
600 ml/1 pint vegetable stock
½ tsp, or to taste, freshly

grated nutmeg
salt and freshly ground
  black pepper
1 tbsp vegetable oil,
  for frying
4 tbsp double cream
warm crusty bread, to serve

Finely chop one of the onions. Melt the butter in a large saucepan and add the chopped onion, carrot, swede, turnips, parsnip and potato. Cover and cook gently for about 10 minutes, without colouring. Stir occasionally during this time.

Add the stock and season to taste with the nutmeg, salt and pepper. Cover and bring to the boil, then reduce the heat and simmer gently for 15–20 minutes, or until the vegetables are tender. Remove from the heat and leave to cool for 30 minutes.

Heat the oil in a large heavy-based frying pan. Thinly slice the remaining onion and cook over a medium heat for about 2–3 minutes, stirring frequently, until crisp and golden brown. Remove the onions with a slotted spoon and drain well on absorbent kitchen paper.

Pour the cooled soup into a food processor or blender and process to form a smooth purée. Return to the cleaned pan, adjust the seasoning, then stir in the cream. Gently reheat and top with the crispy onions. Serve immediately with chunks of bread.

Curried Parsnip Soup

SERVES 2

1 tsp cumin seeds
1 tsp coriander seeds
1 tsp oil
1 small onion, peeled and
   chopped
1 garlic clove, peeled and
   crushed

pinch turmeric
pinch, or to taste, chilli
   powder
1 small cinnamon stick
225 g/8 oz parsnips, peeled
   and chopped
600 ml/1 pint vegetable stock

salt and freshly ground
   black pepper
fresh coriander leaves,
   to garnish
2 tbsp natural yogurt,
   to serve

In a small frying pan, dry-fry the cumin and coriander seeds over a moderately high heat for 1–2 minutes. Shake the pan during cooking until the seeds are lightly toasted.

Reserve until cooled. Grind the toasted seeds in a pestle and mortar.

Heat the oil in a saucepan. Cook the onion until softened and starting to turn golden.

Add the garlic, turmeric, chilli powder and cinnamon stick to the pan. Continue to cook for a further minute.

Add the parsnips and stir well. Pour in the stock and bring to the boil. Cover and simmer for 15 minutes, or until the parsnips are cooked.

Allow the soup to cool. Once cooled, remove the cinnamon stick and discard.

Blend the soup in a food processor until very smooth.

Transfer to a saucepan and reheat gently. Season to taste with salt and pepper. Garnish with fresh coriander and serve immediately with the yogurt.

Lettuce Soup

SERVES 2

1 iceberg lettuce, quartered
   with hard core removed
1 tbsp olive oil
2 tbsp butter
6, about 25 g/1 oz, spring
   onions, trimmed
   and chopped

1 tbsp freshly chopped
   parsley
2 tsp plain flour
600 ml/1 pint chicken stock
salt and freshly ground
   black pepper
4 tbsp single cream

¼ tsp, or to taste, cayenne
   pepper
thick slices stale
   ciabatta bread
parsley sprigs, to garnish

Bring a large saucepan of water to the boil and blanch the lettuce leaves for 3 minutes. Drain and dry thoroughly on absorbent kitchen paper, then shred with a sharp knife.

Heat the oil and butter in a clean saucepan and add the lettuce, spring onions and parsley and cook together for 3–4 minutes, or until very soft.

Stir in the flour and cook for 1 minute, then gradually pour in the stock, stirring throughout. Bring to the boil and season to taste with salt and pepper. Reduce the heat, cover and simmer gently for 10–15 minutes, or until soft.

Allow the soup to cool slightly, then either sieve or purée in a blender. Alternatively, leave the soup chunky. Stir in the cream, add more seasoning, to taste, if liked, then add the cayenne pepper.

Arrange the slices of ciabatta bread in a large soup dish or in individual bowls and pour the soup over the bread. Garnish with sprigs of parsley and serve immediately.

HELPFUL HINT

If a thicker soup is preferred, reduce the amount of stock to 400 ml/14 fl oz.

Hot & Sour Mushroom Soup

SERVES 2

1–2 tbsp sunflower oil
1–2 garlic cloves, peeled
    and finely chopped
2 shallots, peeled and finely
    chopped
2 large red chillies,
    deseeded and finely
    chopped
1 tsp soft brown sugar

pinch salt
600 ml/1 pint vegetable stock
75 g/3 oz Thai fragrant rice
2 kaffir lime leaves, torn
1 tbsp soy sauce
grated zest and juice of
    1 lemon
175 g/6 oz oyster mushrooms,
    wiped and cut into pieces

1 tbsp freshly chopped
    coriander

To garnish:
1 green chilli, deseeded and
    finely chopped
1 large spring onion, trimmed
    and finely chopped

Heat the oil in a frying pan, add the garlic and shallots and cook until golden brown and starting to crisp. Remove from the pan and reserve. Add the chillies to the pan and cook until they start to change colour.

Place the garlic, shallots and chillies in a food processor or blender and blend to a smooth purée with 150 ml/¼ pint water. Pour the purée back into the pan, add the sugar with a large pinch salt, then cook gently, stirring, until dark in colour. Take care not to burn the mixture.

Pour the stock into a large saucepan, add the garlic purée, rice, lime leaves, soy sauce and the lemon zest and juice. Bring to the boil, then reduce the heat, cover and simmer gently for about 10 minutes.

Add the mushrooms and simmer for a further 10 minutes, or until the mushrooms and rice are tender. Remove the lime leaves, stir in the chopped coriander and ladle into bowls. Place the chopped green chilli and spring onions in small bowls and serve separately to sprinkle on top of the soup.

Bacon & Split Pea Soup

SERVES 2

25 g/1 oz dried green or yellow split peas
1 tbsp butter
1 garlic clove, peeled and finely chopped
1 small onion, peeled and thinly sliced
75 g/3 oz long-grain rice

1 tbsp tomato purée
600 ml/1 pint vegetable or chicken stock
1 carrot, about 50 g/2 oz in weight, peeled and finely diced
50 g/2 oz streaky bacon, finely chopped

salt and freshly ground black pepper
1 tbsp freshly chopped parsley
2 tbsp single cream
warm crusty garlic bread, to serve

Cover the dried split peas with plenty of cold water, cover loosely and leave to soak for a minimum of 12 hours, preferably overnight.

Melt the butter in a heavy-based saucepan, add the garlic and onion and cook for 2–3 minutes, without colouring. Add the rice, drained split peas and tomato purée and cook for 2–3 minutes, stirring constantly to prevent sticking. Add the stock, bring to the boil, then reduce the heat and simmer for 20–25 minutes, or until the rice and peas are tender. Remove from the heat and leave to cool.

Blend about three-quarters of the soup in a food processor or blender to form a smooth purée. Pour the purée into the remaining soup in the saucepan. Add the carrot to the saucepan and cook for a further 10–12 minutes, or until the carrot is tender.

Meanwhile, place the bacon in a nonstick frying pan and cook over a gentle heat until the bacon is crisp. Remove and drain on absorbent kitchen paper.

Season the soup with salt and pepper, then stir in the parsley and cream. Reheat for 2–3 minutes, then ladle into bowls. Sprinkle with the bacon and serve with warm garlic bread.

HELPFUL HINT

For a quicker alternative, use red split lentils as they are quick to cook and do not need pre-soaking.

White Bean Soup with Parmesan Croutons

SERVES 2

1 thick slice white bread, cut into 1 cm/½ inch cubes
1 tbsp groundnut oil
1 tbsp finely grated Parmesan cheese
1 tbsp light olive oil
1 small onion, peeled and finely chopped

25 g/1 oz unsmoked bacon lardons (or thick slices bacon, diced)
1 tbsp fresh thyme leaves
1 x 400 g can cannellini beans, drained
600 ml/1 pint chicken stock
salt and freshly ground

black pepper
1 tbsp prepared pesto sauce
25 g/1 oz piece pepperoni sausage, diced
1 tbsp fresh lemon juice
1 tbsp fresh basil, roughly shredded

Preheat oven to 200°C/400°F/Gas Mark 6. Place the cubes of bread in a bowl and pour over the groundnut oil. Stir to coat the bread, then sprinkle over the Parmesan cheese. Place on a lightly oiled baking tray and bake in the preheated oven for 10 minutes, or until crisp and golden.

Heat the olive oil in a large saucepan and cook the onion for 4–5 minutes until softened. Add the bacon and thyme and cook for a further 3 minutes. Stir in the beans, stock and black pepper and simmer gently for 5 minutes.

Place half the bean mixture and liquid into a food processor and blend until smooth.

Return the purée to the saucepan. Stir in the pesto sauce, pepperoni sausage and lemon juice and season to taste with salt and pepper.

Return the soup to the heat and cook for a further 2–3 minutes, or until piping hot. Meanwhile, heat the remaining beans until hot, then place into two warm serving bowls. Add a ladleful of soup. Garnish with shredded basil and serve immediately with the croutons scattered over the top.

Tuna Chowder

SERVES 2

2 tsp vegetable oil
1 small onion, peeled and
    finely chopped
1 celery stalk, trimmed and
    finely sliced
1 tbsp plain flour

350 ml/12 fl oz skimmed milk
125 g/4 oz canned tuna
    in water
50 g/2 oz sweetcorn, canned
    in water or frozen; drained
    or thawed

1 tsp freshly chopped thyme
salt and freshly ground
    black pepper
pinch cayenne pepper
1 tbsp freshly chopped
    parsley

Heat the oil in a heavy-based saucepan. Add the onion and celery and cook gently for about 5 minutes, stirring from time to time, until the onion is softened.

Stir in the flour and cook for about 1 minute to thicken.

Draw the pan off the heat and gradually pour in the milk, stirring throughout.

Add the tuna and its liquid, the sweetcorn and the thyme.

Mix gently, then bring to the boil. Cover and simmer for 5 minutes.

Remove the pan from the heat and season to taste with salt and pepper.

Sprinkle the chowder with the cayenne pepper and chopped parsley.
Divide into soup bowls and serve immediately.

TASTY TIP

If using canned sweetcorn, transfer the remaining kernels into a small dish, cover and keep for up to 2 days in the refrigerator.

Creamy Caribbean Chicken & Coconut Soup

SERVES 2

4–5 spring onions
1 garlic clove
1 red chilli
125 g/4 oz cooked chicken,
   shredded or diced
2 tsp vegetable oil
scant 1 tsp ground turmeric

125 ml/4 fl oz coconut milk
350 ml/12 fl oz chicken stock
25 g/1 oz small soup pasta
   or spaghetti, broken into
   small pieces
2 lemon slices
salt and freshly ground

black pepper
1–2 tbsp freshly chopped
   coriander
fresh coriander sprigs,
   to garnish

Trim the spring onions and slice thinly; peel the garlic and chop finely. Cut off the top from the chilli, slit down the side and remove seeds and membrane, then chop finely and reserve.

Remove and discard any skin or bones from the cooked chicken and shred using 2 forks and reserve.

Heat a large wok, add the oil and, when hot, add the spring onions, garlic and chilli and stir-fry for 2 minutes, or until the onion has softened. Stir in the turmeric and cook for 1 minute.

Blend the coconut milk with the chicken stock until smooth, then pour into the wok. Add the pasta or spaghetti with the lemon slices and bring to the boil.

Simmer, half-covered, for 10–12 minutes, or until the pasta is tender; stir occasionally.

Remove the lemon slices from the wok and add the chicken. Season to taste with salt and pepper and simmer for 2–3 minutes, or until the chicken is heated through thoroughly.

Stir in the chopped coriander and ladle into heated bowls. Garnish with sprigs of fresh coriander and serve immediately.

Creamy Salmon
with Dill in Filo Baskets

SERVES 2

1 bay leaf
4 black peppercorns
1 large sprig fresh parsley
125 g/4 oz salmon fillet

2 large sheets filo pastry
fine spray of olive oil
50 g/2 oz baby spinach leaves
2 tbsp fromage frais

1 tsp Dijon mustard
2 tbsp freshly chopped dill
salt and freshly ground black
    pepper

Preheat the oven to 200°C/400°F/Gas Mark 6. Place the bay leaf, peppercorns, parsley and salmon in a frying pan and add enough water to barely cover the fish.

Bring to the boil, reduce the heat and poach the fish for 5 minutes until it flakes easily. Remove it from the pan. Reserve.

Spray each sheet of filo pastry lightly with the oil. Scrunch up the pastry to make a nest shape approximately 12.5 cm/5 inches in diameter.

Place on a lightly oiled baking sheet and cook in the preheated oven for 10 minutes until golden and crisp.

Blanch the spinach in a pan of lightly salted boiling water for 2 minutes. Drain thoroughly and keep warm.

Mix the fromage frais, mustard and dill together, then warm gently. Season to taste with salt and pepper. Divide the spinach between the filo pastry nests and flake the salmon onto the spinach.

Spoon the mustard and dill sauce over the filo baskets and serve immediately.

Sweet-&-Sour Battered Fish

SERVES 2

275 g/10 oz cod fillet,
  skinned
75 g/3 oz plain flour
salt and freshly ground
  black pepper
1 tbsp cornflour
1 tbsp arrowroot

vegetable oil, for deep-frying

For the sweet-&-sour sauce:
2 tbsp orange juice
1 tbsp white wine vinegar
1 tbsp dry sherry
1 tbsp dark soy sauce

1 tbsp, or to taste, soft light
  brown sugar
1 tsp tomato purée
½ small red pepper,
  deseeded and diced
1 tsp cornflour

Cut the fish into pieces about 5 x 2.5 cm/2 x 1 inch. Place 2 tablespoons of the flour in a small bowl, season with salt and pepper to taste, then add the fish pieces a few at a time and toss until coated.

Sift the remaining flour into a bowl with a pinch salt, the cornflour and arrowroot. Gradually whisk in about 150 ml/¼ pint iced water to make a smooth, thin batter.

Heat the oil in a wok or deep-fat fryer to 190˚C/375˚F. Working in batches, dip the fish in the batter allowing any excess to drip back into the bowl. Deep-fry them for 3–5 minutes, or until crisp. Using a slotted spoon, remove the fish and drain on absorbent kitchen paper.

Meanwhile, make the sauce. Place 1 tablespoon of the orange juice, the vinegar, sherry, soy sauce, sugar, tomato purée and red pepper in a small saucepan. Bring to the boil, lower the heat and simmer for 2 minutes.

Blend the cornflour with the remaining orange juice, stir into the sauce and simmer, stirring, for 1 minute, or until thickened. Arrange the fish on a warmed platter or individual plates. Drizzle a little of the sauce over and serve immediately with the remaining sauce.

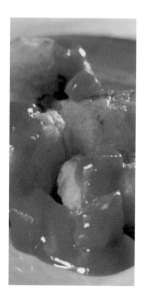

Thai Fish Cakes

SERVES 2

1 red chilli, deseeded and
   roughly chopped
2 tbsp roughly chopped
   fresh coriander
1 garlic clove, peeled and
   crushed
2 spring onions, trimmed

and roughly chopped
1 lemon grass stalk, outer
   leaves discarded,
   and roughly chopped
50 g/2 oz prawns,
   thawed if frozen
150 g/5 oz cod fillet, skinned,

pin bones removed
   and cubed
salt and freshly ground
   black pepper
sweet chilli dipping sauce,
   to serve

Preheat the oven to 190°C/375°F/Gas Mark 5. Place the chilli, coriander, garlic, spring onions and lemon grass in a food processor and blend together.

Pat the prawns and cod dry with kitchen paper.

Add to the food processor and blend until the mixture is roughly chopped.

Season to taste with salt and pepper and blend to mix.

Dampen the hands, then shape heaped tablespoons of the mixture into 12 little fish cakes.

Place the fish cakes on a lightly oiled baking sheet and cook in the preheated oven for 12–15 minutes, or until piping hot and cooked through. Turn them over halfway through the cooking time.

Serve the fish cakes immediately with the sweet chilli sauce for dipping.

Fried Whitebait with Rocket Salad

SERVES 2

125 g/4 oz whitebait, fresh or frozen
vegetable oil, for frying
50 g/2 oz plain flour
½ tsp, or to taste, cayenne pepper
salt and freshly ground

black pepper

For the salad:
75 g/3 oz rocket leaves
75 g/3 oz cherry tomatoes, halved
50 g/2 oz cucumber, cut

into dice
2 tbsp olive oil
1 tbsp fresh lemon juice
½ tsp Dijon mustard
½ tsp caster sugar

If the whitebait are frozen, thaw completely, then pat dry with absorbent kitchen paper.

Start to heat the oil in a deep-fat fryer. Arrange the fish in a large shallow dish and toss well in the flour, cayenne pepper and salt and pepper.

Deep-fry the fish in batches for 2–3 minutes, or until crisp and golden. Keep the cooked fish warm while deep-frying the remaining fish.

Meanwhile, to make the salad, arrange the rocket leaves, cherry tomatoes and cucumber on individual serving dishes. Whisk the olive oil and the remaining ingredients together and season lightly. Drizzle the dressing over the salad and serve with the whitebait.

TASTY TIP

Why not try a different salad? Mix together some cleaned baby spinach, cooled, cooked petits pois and chopped spring onions, then pour over 2 tablespoons of garlic olive oil.

Quick Mediterranean Prawns

SERVES 2

16 raw Mediterranean
    prawns
2 tbsp olive oil
1 garlic clove, peeled and
    crushed
finely grated zest and juice
    of ½ lemon

fresh rosemary sprigs

**For the pesto and sun-dried
    tomato dips:**
150 ml/¼ pint Greek-style
    yogurt
1 tbsp prepared pesto

150 ml/¼ pint crème fraîche
1 tbsp sun-dried tomato paste
1 tbsp wholegrain mustard
salt and freshly ground
    black pepper
lemon wedges, to garnish

Remove the shells from the prawns, leaving the tail shells intact. Using a small, sharp knife, remove the black vein that runs along the backs of the prawns. Rinse and drain on absorbent kitchen paper.

Whisk 1 tablespoon of the oil with the garlic, lemon zest and juice in a small bowl. Bruise 1 sprig of rosemary with a rolling pin and add to the bowl. Add the prawns, toss to coat, then cover and leave to marinate in the refrigerator until needed.

For the simple dips, mix the yogurt and pesto in one bowl and the crème fraîche, tomato paste and mustard in another bowl. Season to taste with salt and pepper.

Heat a wok, add the remaining oil and swirl round to coat the sides. Remove the prawns from the marinade, leaving any juices and the rosemary behind. Add to the wok and stir-fry over a high heat for 3–4 minutes, or until the prawns are pink and just cooked through.

Remove the prawns from the wok and arrange on a platter. Garnish with lemon wedges and more fresh rosemary sprigs and serve hot or cold with the dips.

Sesame Prawns

SERVES 2

16 large raw prawns
2 tbsp plain flour
2 tbsp sesame seeds
salt and freshly ground
    black pepper
1 large egg

300 ml/½ pint vegetable oil,
    for deep-frying

For the soy dipping sauce:
50 ml/2 fl oz soy sauce
1 spring onion, trimmed and

    finely chopped
½ tsp dried crushed chillies
1 tbsp sesame oil
1–2 tsp sugar, or to taste
spring onion strips,
    to garnish

Remove the heads from the prawns by twisting away from the body and discard. Peel the prawns, leaving the tails on for presentation. Using a sharp knife, remove the black vein from the back of the prawns. Rinse and pat dry. Slice along the back, but do not cut through the prawn body. Place on the chopping board and press firmly to flatten slightly, to make a butterfly shape.

Put the flour, half the sesame seeds, salt and pepper into a food processor and blend for 30 seconds. Tip into a polythene bag and add the prawns, 4–5 at a time. Twist to seal, then shake to coat with the flour.

Beat the egg in a small bowl with the remaining sesame seeds, salt and pepper.

Heat the oil in a large wok to 190˚C/375˚F, or until a small cube of bread browns in about 30 seconds. Working in batches of 5 or 6 and holding each prawn by the tail, dip into the beaten egg, allowing any excess to drip back into the bowl, then carefully lower into the oil. Cook for 1–2 minutes, or until crisp and golden, turning once or twice. Using a slotted spoon, remove the prawns, drain on absorbent kitchen paper and keep warm.

For the dipping sauce, stir together the soy sauce, spring onion, chillies, oil and sugar until the sugar dissolves. Arrange the prawns on a plate, garnish with strips of spring onion and serve.

Crispy Prawns with Chinese Dipping Sauce

SERVES 2

225 g/8 oz medium-sized raw prawns, peeled
pinch salt
3–4 tbsp groundnut oil
1–2 garlic cloves, peeled and finely chopped
2.5 cm/1 inch piece fresh

root ginger, peeled and finely chopped
1 green chilli, deseeded and finely chopped
4 stems fresh coriander, leaves and stems roughly chopped

For the Chinese dipping sauce:
1 tbsp dark soy sauce
1 tbsp rice wine vinegar
1 tsp caster sugar
1–2 tbsp chilli oil
2 spring onions, finely shredded

Using a sharp knife, remove the black vein along the back of the prawns. Sprinkle the prawns with the salt and leave to stand for 15 minutes. Rinse the salt off and pat dry on absorbent kitchen paper.

Heat a wok or frying pan, add the groundnut oil and, when hot, add the prawns and stir-fry in 2 batches for about 1 minute, or until they turn pink and are almost cooked. Using a slotted spoon, remove the prawns and keep warm in a low oven.

Drain the oil from the wok, leaving 1 tablespoon. Add the garlic, ginger and chilli and cook for about 30 seconds. Add the coriander, return the prawns and stir-fry for 1–2 minutes, or until the prawns are cooked through and the garlic is golden. Turn into a warmed serving dish.

For the dipping sauce, using a fork, beat together the soy sauce, rice wine vinegar, caster sugar and chilli oil in a small bowl. Stir in the spring onions. Serve immediately with the hot prawns.

Mussels with Creamy Garlic & Saffron Sauce

SERVES 2

450 g/1 lb fresh live mussels
250 ml/8 fl oz good-quality dry white wine
1 tbsp olive oil
1 shallot, peeled and finely chopped
2 garlic cloves, peeled and crushed
1 tbsp freshly chopped oregano
few saffron strands
125 ml/4 fl oz single cream
salt and freshly ground black pepper
fresh crusty bread, to serve

Clean the mussels thoroughly in plenty of cold water and remove any beards and barnacles from the shells. Discard any mussels that are open or damaged. Place in a large bowl, cover with cold water and leave in the refrigerator until required, if prepared earlier.

Pour the wine into a large saucepan and bring to the boil. Tip the mussels into the pan, cover and cook, shaking the saucepan periodically, for 6–8 minutes, or until the mussels have opened completely.

Using a slotted spoon, carefully remove the mussels from the saucepan, discarding any that are closed. Keep warm. Reserve the cooking liquor.

Meanwhile, heat the olive oil in a frying pan and cook the shallot and garlic gently for 2–3 minutes until softened. Add the reserved cooking liquid and chopped oregano and cook for a further 3–4 minutes. Stir in the saffron and the cream and heat through gently. Season to taste with salt and pepper. Place the mussels in individual serving bowls and spoon over the saffron sauce. Serve immediately with plenty of fresh crusty bread.

HELPFUL HINT

Remember, when buying live mussels you will need quite a few even for 2 portions. Most of the weight is made up of the shells, and you need to allow for the mussels which do not open.

Moo Shi Pork

SERVES 2

75 g/3 oz pork fillet
2 tsp Chinese rice wine or
   dry sherry
1 tbsp light soy sauce
1 tsp cornflour
25 g/1 oz dried golden
   needles, soaked and
   drained

2 tbsp groundnut oil
1 large egg, lightly beaten
1 tsp freshly grated
   root ginger
2 spring onions, trimmed
   and thinly sliced
50 g/2 oz bamboo shoots,
   cut into fine strips

salt and freshly ground
   black pepper
4 mandarin pancakes,
   steamed
hoisin sauce
fresh coriander sprigs,
   to garnish

Cut the pork across the grain into 1 cm/½ inch slices, then cut into thin strips. Place in a bowl with the Chinese rice wine or sherry, soy sauce and cornflour. Mix well and reserve. Trim off the tough ends of the golden needles, then cut in half and reserve.

Heat a wok or large frying pan, add 1 tablespoon of the groundnut oil and, when hot, add the lightly beaten egg and cook for 1 minute, stirring all the time, until scrambled. Remove and reserve. Wipe the wok clean with absorbent kitchen paper.

Return the wok to the heat, add the remaining oil and, when hot, transfer the pork strips from the marinade mixture to the wok, shaking off as much marinade as possible. Stir-fry for 30 seconds, then add the ginger, spring onions and bamboo shoots and pour in the marinade. Stir-fry for 2–3 minutes, or until cooked.

Return the scrambled egg to the wok, season to taste with salt and pepper and stir for a few seconds until mixed well and heated through. Divide the mixture between the pancakes, drizzle each with 1 teaspoon of hoisin sauce and roll up. Garnish with fresh coriander sprigs and serve immediately.

Spicy Beef Pancakes

SERVES 2

25 g/1 oz plain flour
pinch salt
½ tsp Chinese five-spice
  powder
1 small egg yolk
65 ml/2½ fl oz milk
2 tsp sunflower oil
slices of spring onion,
  to garnish

For the spicy beef filling:
1 tsp sesame oil
2 spring onions, sliced
1 cm/½ inch piece fresh root
  ginger, peeled and grated
1 garlic clove, peeled and
  crushed
150 g/5 oz sirloin steak,
  trimmed and cut into strips

1 red chilli, deseeded and
  finely chopped
1 tsp sherry vinegar
1 tsp soft dark brown sugar
1 tsp dark soy sauce

Sift the flour, salt and Chinese five-spice powder into a bowl and make a well in the centre. Add the egg yolk and a little of the milk. Gradually beat in, drawing in the flour to make a smooth batter. Whisk in the rest of the milk.

Heat a little of the sunflower oil in a small heavy-based frying pan. Pour in just enough batter to thinly coat the base of the pan. Cook over a medium heat for 1 minute, or until the underside of the pancake is golden brown. Turn or toss the pancake and cook for 1 minute, or until the other side of the pancake is golden brown. Make 3 more pancakes with the remaining batter, adding a little more oil as required. Stack them on a warmed plate as you make them, with greaseproof paper between each pancake. Cover with foil and keep warm in a low oven.

Make the filling. Heat a wok or large frying pan, add the sesame oil and, when hot, add the spring onions, ginger and garlic and stir-fry for 1 minute. Add the beef strips, stir-fry for 3–4 minutes, then stir in the chilli, vinegar, sugar and soy sauce. Cook for 1 minute, then remove from the heat.

Spoon a quarter of the filling over one half of each pancake. Fold the pancakes in half, then fold in half again. Garnish with a few slices of spring onion and serve immediately.

Oriental Minced Chicken on Rocket & Tomato

SERVES 2

1 shallot, peeled
1 garlic clove, peeled
1 small carrot, peeled
25 g/1 oz water chestnuts
1 tsp vegetable oil

175 g/6 oz fresh chicken mince
1 tsp Chinese five-spice powder
pinch chilli powder

1 tsp soy sauce
1 tsp fish sauce
4–6 cherry tomatoes
25 g/1 oz rocket

Finely chop the shallot and garlic. Cut the carrot into matchsticks, thinly slice the water chestnuts and reserve. Heat the oil in a wok or large heavy-based frying pan and add the chicken. Stir-fry for 3–4 minutes over a moderately high heat, breaking up any large pieces of chicken.

Add the garlic and shallot and cook for 2–3 minutes until softened. Sprinkle over the Chinese five-spice powder and the chilli powder and continue to cook for about 1 minute.

Add the carrot, water chestnuts, soy and fish sauce, and 1 tablespoon water. Stir-fry for a further 2 minutes. Remove from the heat and reserve to cool slightly.

Deseed the tomatoes and cut into thin wedges. Toss with the rocket and divide between 2 serving plates. Spoon the warm chicken mixture over the rocket and tomato wedges and serve immediately to prevent the rocket from wilting.

TASTY TIP

In place of the chicken you could use any lean cut of meat or even prawns. To make this dish a main meal replace the rocket and tomatoes with stir-fried vegetables and rice.

Hoisin Chicken Pancakes

SERVES 2

3 tbsp hoisin sauce
1 garlic clove, peeled and
    crushed
2.5 cm/1 inch piece root
    ginger, peeled and
    finely grated
1 tbsp soy sauce

1 tsp sesame oil
salt and freshly ground
    black pepper
2 skinless chicken thighs
¼–½, depending on size,
    cucumber, peeled
    (optional)

6 bought Chinese pancakes
3 spring onions, trimmed
    and cut lengthways into
    fine shreds
sweet chilli dipping sauce,
    to serve

Preheat the oven to 190°C/375°F/Gas Mark 5. In a nonmetallic bowl, mix the hoisin sauce with the garlic, ginger, soy sauce, sesame oil and seasoning.

Add the chicken thighs and turn to coat in the mixture. Cover loosely and leave in the refrigerator to marinate for 3–4 hours, turning the chicken from time to time.

Remove the chicken from the marinade and place in a roasting tin. Reserve the marinade. Bake in the preheated oven for 30 minutes, basting occasionally with the marinade.

Cut the cucumber in half lengthways and remove the seeds by running a teaspoon down the middle to scoop them out. Cut into thin batons.

Place the pancakes in a steamer to warm or heat, according to packet instructions. Thinly slice the hot chicken and arrange on a plate with the shredded spring onions, cucumber and pancakes.

Place a spoonful of the chicken in the middle of each warmed pancake and top with pieces of cucumber, spring onion and a little dipping sauce. Roll up and serve immediately.

TASTY TIP

To make this more substantial, stir-fry the spring onions and cucumber batons in a little groundnut oil. Add a carrot cut into batons and mix in the sliced chicken and reserved marinade. Serve with rice.

Chicken–filled Spring Rolls

MAKES 6 ROLLS

For the filling:
1 tbsp vegetable oil
1 rasher streaky bacon, rind
    removed, and chopped
75 g/3 oz skinless chicken
    breast fillets, thinly sliced
½ small red pepper,
    deseeded and finely
    chopped
2 spring onions, trimmed

and finely chopped
2 tsp freshly grated root
    ginger
25 g/1 oz mangetout,
    thinly sliced
25 g/1 oz beansprouts
1 tsp soy sauce
1 tsp Chinese rice wine
    or dry sherry
1 tsp hoisin or plum sauce

For the wrappers:
1½ tbsp plain flour
6 spring roll wrappers
300 ml/½ pint vegetable oil,
    for deep-frying
shredded spring onions,
    to garnish
dipping sauce, to serve

Heat a large wok, add the oil and, when hot, add the diced bacon and stir-fry for 2–3 minutes, or until golden. Add the chicken and pepper and stir-fry for a further 2–3 minutes. Add the remaining filling ingredients and stir-fry for 3–4 minutes until all the vegetables are tender. Turn into a colander and leave to drain as the mixture cools completely.

Blend the flour with about 2–3 teaspoons of water to form a paste. Soften each wrapper in a plate of warm water for 1–2 seconds, then place on a chopping board. Put 2–3 tablespoons of filling on the near edge. Fold the other edge over the filling to cover. Fold in each side and roll up. Seal the edge with a little flour paste and press to seal securely. Transfer to a baking sheet, seam-side down.

HELPFUL HINT
Make extra spring rolls and freeze, then serve when friends or family come round.

Heat the oil in a large wok to 190°C/375°F, or until a small cube of bread browns in about 30 seconds. Working in batches, fry the spring rolls until they are crisp and golden, turning once (about 2 minutes). Remove and drain on absorbent kitchen paper. Arrange the spring rolls on a serving plate, garnish with spring onion tassels and serve hot with the dipping sauce.

Shredded Duck in Lettuce Leaves

SERVES 2

15 g/½ oz dried Chinese (shiitake) mushrooms
1 tbsp vegetable oil
200 g/7 oz boneless, skinless duck breast, cut crossways into thin strips
1 red chilli, deseeded and thinly sliced diagonally

3 spring onions, trimmed and diagonally sliced
1–2 garlic cloves, peeled and crushed
40 g/1½ oz beansprouts
1 tbsp soy sauce
1 tbsp Chinese rice wine or dry sherry

1–2 tsp clear honey or brown sugar
2 tbsp hoisin sauce
large crisp lettuce leaves such as iceberg or cos
handful of fresh mint leaves
dipping sauce (*see* Sesame Prawns, page 74)

Cover the dried Chinese mushrooms with almost boiling water, leave for 20 minutes, then drain and slice thinly.

Heat a large wok, add the oil and, when hot, stir-fry the duck for 3–4 minutes, or until sealed. Remove with a slotted spoon and reserve.

Add the chilli, spring onions, garlic and Chinese mushrooms to the wok and stir-fry for 2–3 minutes, or until softened.

Add the beansprouts, soy sauce, Chinese rice wine or dry sherry and honey or brown sugar to the wok and continue to stir-fry for 1 minute, or until blended.

Stir in the reserved duck and stir-fry for 2 minutes, or until well mixed together and heated right through. Transfer to a heated serving dish.

Arrange the hoisin and dipping sauces in small bowls on a tray or plate with a pile of lettuce leaves and the mint leaves.

Roasted Aubergine Dip with Pitta Strips

SERVES 2

2 pitta breads
2 aubergines
1 garlic clove, peeled
¼ tsp sesame oil

1 tsp lemon juice
½ tsp ground cumin
salt and freshly ground
   black pepper

1 tbsp freshly chopped
   parsley
fresh salad leaves, to serve

Preheat the oven to 180°C/350°F/Gas Mark 4. On a chopping board, cut the pitta breads into strips. Spread the bread in a single layer onto a large baking tray.

Cook in the preheated oven for 15 minutes until golden and crisp. Leave to cool on a wire cooling rack.

Trim the aubergines, rinse lightly and reserve. Heat a griddle pan until almost smoking. Cook the aubergines and garlic for about 15 minutes.

Turn the aubergines frequently, until very tender with wrinkled and charred skins. Remove from the heat and leave to cool.

When the aubergines are cool enough to handle, cut in half and scoop out the cooked flesh and place in a food processor.

Squeeze the softened garlic flesh from the papery skin and add to the aubergine. Blend the aubergine and garlic until smooth, then add the sesame oil, lemon juice and cumin and blend again to mix.

Season to taste with salt and pepper, stir in the parsley and serve with the pitta strips and mixed salad leaves.

Bruschetta with Pecorino, Garlic & Tomatoes

SERVES 2

3 ripe but firm tomatoes
50 g/2 oz pecorino cheese,
   finely grated
2 tsp oregano leaves
salt and freshly ground
   black pepper

2–3 tbsp olive oil
2 garlic cloves, peeled
4 slices of Italian flatbread,
   such as focaccia
25 g/1 oz mozzarella cheese
marinated black olives,

to serve
mixed salad leaves (such as
   frisée, radicchio and
   rocket), to serve (optional)

Preheat the grill and line the grill rack with kitchen foil just before cooking. Make a small cross in the tops of the tomatoes, then place in a small bowl and cover with boiling water. Leave to stand for 2 minutes, then drain and remove the skins. Cut into quarters, remove the seeds and chop the flesh into small dice.

Mix the tomato flesh with the pecorino cheese and 1 teaspoon of the fresh oregano and season to taste with salt and pepper. Add 1 tablespoon of the olive oil and mix thoroughly.

Crush the garlic and spread evenly over the slices of bread. Heat half the remaining olive oil in a large frying pan and sauté the bread slices until they are crisp and golden, adding more oil if necessary.

Place the fried bread on a lightly oiled baking tray and spoon on the tomato and cheese topping. Place a little mozzarella on top and place under the preheated grill for 3–4 minutes, until golden and bubbling. Garnish with the remaining oregano, then arrange the bruschettas on a serving plate and serve immediately with the olives and the salad leaves (if using).

Pasta with Walnut Sauce

SERVES 2

25 g/1 oz walnuts, toasted
2 spring onions, trimmed
   and chopped
1–2 garlic cloves, peeled
   and sliced

1 tsp freshly chopped
   parsley or basil
3 tbsp extra-virgin olive oil
salt and freshly ground
   black pepper

225 g/8 oz broccoli, cut
   into florets
175 g/6 oz pasta shapes
1 red chilli, deseeded and
   finely chopped

Place the toasted walnuts in a blender or food processor with the chopped spring onions, half the garlic and parsley or basil. Blend to a fairly smooth paste, then gradually add two tablespoons of the olive oil, until it is well mixed into the paste. Season the walnut paste to taste with salt and pepper and reserve.

Bring a large pan of lightly salted water to a rolling boil. Add the broccoli, return to the boil and cook for 2 minutes. Remove the broccoli using a slotted spoon and refresh under cold running water. Drain again and pat dry on absorbent kitchen paper.

Bring the water back to a rolling boil. Add the pasta and cook according to the packet instructions, or until *al dente*.

Meanwhile, heat the remaining oil in a frying pan. Add the remaining garlic and the chilli. Cook gently for 2 minutes, or until softened. Add the broccoli and walnut paste. Cook for a further 3–4 minutes, or until heated through.

Drain the pasta thoroughly and transfer to a large warmed serving bowl. Pour over the walnut and broccoli mixture. Toss together, adjust the seasoning and serve immediately.

Tagliarini with Broad Beans, Saffron & Crème Fraîche

SERVES 2

225 g/8 oz fresh young
broad beans in pods or
100 g/3½ oz frozen broad
beans, thawed
1 tbsp olive oil
1 garlic clove, peeled

and chopped
small handful basil leaves,
shredded
200 ml/7 fl oz crème fraîche
large pinch saffron strands
300 g/10 oz tagliarini

salt and freshly ground
black pepper
1 tbsp freshly snipped chives
freshly grated Parmesan
cheese, to serve

If using fresh broad beans, bring a pan of lightly salted water to the boil. Pod the beans and drop them into the boiling water for 1 minute. Drain and refresh under cold water. Drain again. Remove the outer skins of the beans and discard. If using thawed frozen broad beans, remove and discard the skins. Reserve the peeled beans.

Heat the olive oil in a saucepan. Add the peeled broad beans and the garlic and cook gently for 2–3 minutes. Stir in the basil, the crème fraîche and the saffron strands and simmer for 1 minute.

Meanwhile, bring a large pan of lightly salted water to a rolling boil. Add the pasta and cook according to the packet instructions, or until *al dente*. Drain the pasta well and add to the sauce. Toss together and season to taste with salt and pepper.

Transfer the pasta and sauce to a warmed serving dish. Sprinkle with snipped chives and serve immediately with Parmesan cheese.

Tortellini, Cherry Tomato & Mozzarella Skewers

SERVES 2

125 g/4 oz mixed green and plain cheese or vegetable-filled fresh tortellini
6 tbsp extra-virgin olive oil
2 garlic cloves, peeled

and crushed
pinch dried thyme or basil
salt and freshly ground black pepper
12 cherry tomatoes

125 g/4 oz mozzarella, cut into 2.5 cm/1 inch cubes
basil leaves, to garnish
dressed salad leaves, to serve

If using wooden skewers for this recipe, soak them in cold water for at least 30 minutes before cooking to prevent them scorching under the grill. The tips of the skewers may be protected with small pieces of foil. Preheat the grill and line a grill pan with kitchen foil, just before cooking. Bring a large pan of lightly salted water to a rolling boil. Add the tortellini and cook according to the packet instructions, or until *al dente*. Drain, rinse under cold running water, drain again and toss with 1 tablespoon of the olive oil and reserve.

Pour the remaining olive oil into a small bowl. Add the crushed garlic and thyme or basil, then blend well. Season to taste with salt and black pepper and reserve.

To assemble the skewers, thread the tortellini alternately with the cherry tomatoes and cubes of mozzarella. Arrange the skewers on the grill pan and brush generously on all sides with the olive oil mixture.

Cook the skewers under the preheated grill for about 5 minutes, or until they begin to turn golden, turning them halfway through cooking. Arrange 2 skewers on each plate and garnish with a few basil leaves. Serve immediately with dressed salad leaves.

Fish & Seafood

Gingered Cod Steaks

SERVES 2

1 cm/½ inch piece fresh root
   ginger, peeled
4 spring onions
2 tsp freshly chopped parsley
2 tsp soft brown sugar

2 x 175 g/6 oz thick cod
   steaks (or salmon or
   fresh haddock)
salt and freshly ground
   black pepper

1 tbsp butter
freshly cooked vegetables,
   to serve

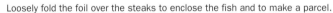

Preheat the grill and line the grill rack with a layer of kitchen foil. Coarsely grate the piece of ginger. Trim the spring onions and cut into thin strips.

Mix the spring onions, ginger, chopped parsley and sugar. Add 1 tablespoon of water.

Wipe the fish steaks. Season to taste with salt and pepper. Place onto 4 separate 20.5 x 20.5 cm/8 x 8 inch foil squares.

Carefully spoon the spring onions and ginger mixture over the fish.

Cut the butter into small cubes and place over the fish.

Loosely fold the foil over the steaks to enclose the fish and to make a parcel.

Place under the preheated grill and cook for 10–12 minutes, or until cooked and the flesh has turned opaque.

Place the fish parcels on individual serving plates. Serve immediately with the freshly cooked vegetables.

Spicy Cod Rice

1 tbsp plain flour
1 tbsp freshly chopped
  coriander
1 tsp ground cumin
1 tsp ground coriander
300 g/10 oz thick-cut cod
  fillet, skinned and cut

into chunks
4 tbsp groundnut oil
50 g/2 oz cashew nuts
4 spring onions, trimmed
  and diagonally sliced
1 red chilli, deseeded and
  chopped

1 carrot, peeled and cut
  into matchsticks
75 g/3 oz frozen peas
225 g/8 oz cooked
  long-grain rice
2 tbsp sweet chilli sauce
2 tbsp soy sauce

Mix together the flour, coriander, cumin and ground coriander on a large plate. Coat the cod in the spice mixture, then place on a baking sheet, cover and chill in the refrigerator for 30 minutes.

Heat a large wok, then add 2 tablespoons of the oil and heat until almost smoking. Stir-fry the cashew nuts for 1 minute until browned, then remove and reserve.

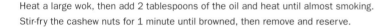

Add a further 1 tablespoon of the oil and heat until almost smoking. Add the cod and stir-fry for 2 minutes. Using a fish slice, turn the cod chunks over and cook for a further 2 minutes until golden. Remove from the wok, place on a warm plate and cover. Add the remaining oil to the wok, heat until almost smoking, then stir-fry the spring onions and chilli for 1 minute before adding the carrots and peas and stir-frying for a further 2 minutes. Stir in the rice, chilli sauce, soy sauce and cashew nuts and stir-fry for 3 more minutes. Add the cod, heat for 1 minute, then serve immediately.

Battered Cod & Chunky Chips

SERVES 2

10 g/¼ oz fresh yeast
150 ml/¼ pint beer
125 g/4 oz plain flour
½ tsp salt
350 g/12 oz potatoes
450 ml/¾ pint groundnut oil

2 cod fillets, about 225 g/8 oz
    each, skinned and boned
1 tbsp seasoned plain flour

To garnish:
lemon wedges

flat-leaf parsley sprigs

To serve:
tomato ketchup
vinegar

Dissolve the yeast with a little of the beer in a jug and mix to a paste. Pour in the remaining beer, whisking all the time until smooth. Place the flour and salt in a bowl and gradually pour in the beer mixture, whisking continuously to make a thick smooth batter. Cover the bowl and allow the batter to stand at room temperature for 1 hour.

Peel the potatoes and cut into thick slices. Cut each slice lengthways to make chunky chips. Place them in a nonstick frying pan and heat, shaking the pan, until all the moisture has evaporated. Turn them onto absorbent kitchen paper to dry off.

Heat the oil to 180°C/350°F, then fry the chips a few at a time for 4–5 minutes until crisp and golden. Drain on absorbent kitchen paper and keep warm.

Pat the cod fillets dry, then coat in the flour. Dip the floured fillets into the reserved batter. Fry for 2–3 minutes until cooked and crisp, then drain. Garnish with lemon wedges and parsley and serve immediately with the chips, tomato ketchup and vinegar.

HELPFUL HINT

Fresh yeast should be moist and creamy-coloured, with a strong yeasty smell. Store it well-wrapped in the refrigerator for up to 3 days. It can be frozen, but should be used within 3 months.

Teriyaki Salmon

SERVES 2

225 g/8 oz salmon fillet, skinned
4 tbsp Japanese teriyaki sauce
1 tbsp rice wine vinegar
2 tsp tomato paste

dash Tabasco sauce
grated zest of ½ lemon
salt and freshly ground black pepper
3 tbsp groundnut oil
1 carrot, peeled and cut into

matchsticks
75 g/3 oz mangetout
75 g/3 oz oyster mushrooms, wiped

Using a sharp knife, cut the salmon into thick slices and place in a shallow dish. Mix together the teriyaki sauce, rice wine vinegar, tomato paste, Tabasco sauce, lemon zest and seasoning. Spoon the marinade over the salmon, then cover loosely and leave to marinate in the refrigerator for 30 minutes, turning the salmon or spooning the marinade occasionally over the salmon.

Heat a large wok, then add 2 tablespoons of the oil until almost smoking. Stir-fry the carrot for 2 minutes, then add the mangetout and stir-fry for a further 2 minutes. Add the oyster mushrooms and stir-fry for 4 minutes until softened. Using a slotted spoon, transfer the vegetables to 2 warmed serving plates and keep warm.

Remove the salmon from the marinade, reserving both the salmon and marinade. Add the remaining oil to the wok, heat until almost smoking, then cook the salmon for 4–5 minutes, turning once during cooking, or until the fish is just flaking. Add the marinade and heat through for 1 minute. Serve immediately, with the salmon arranged on top of the vegetables and the marinade drizzled over.

HELPFUL HINT

Don't forget to use your freezer to take advantage of the supermarkets' special offers on meat and fish, remembering to freeze portions separately.

Pan–fried Salmon with Herb Risotto

SERVES 2

2 x 175 g/6 oz salmon fillets
2 tbsp plain flour
1 tsp dried mustard powder
salt and freshly ground
    black pepper
2 tbsp olive oil
2 shallots, peeled
    and chopped

125 g/4 oz Arborio rice
150 ml/¼ pint dry white wine
600–750 ml/1–1¼ pints
    vegetable or fish stock
25 g/1 oz butter
1 tbsp freshly snipped chives
1 tbsp freshly chopped dill
1 tbsp freshly chopped flat-

leaf parsley
knob of butter

To garnish:
slices of lemon
fresh dill sprigs
tomato salad, to serve

Wipe the salmon fillets with a clean, damp cloth. Mix together the flour, mustard powder and seasoning on a large plate and use to coat the salmon fillets and reserve.

Heat half the olive oil in a large frying pan and fry the shallots for 5 minutes until softened, but not coloured. Add the rice and stir for 1 minute, then slowly add the wine, bring to the boil and boil rapidly until reduced by half.

Bring the stock to a gentle simmer, then add to the rice, a ladleful at a time. Cook, stirring frequently, until all the stock has been added and the rice is cooked but still retains a bite. Stir in the butter and freshly chopped herbs and season to taste with salt and pepper.

Heat the remaining olive oil and the knob of butter in a large griddle pan, add the salmon fillets and cook for 2–3 minutes on each side, or until cooked. Arrange the herb risotto on warm serving plates and top with the salmon. Garnish with slices of lemon and sprigs of dill and serve immediately with a tomato salad.

Seared Salmon & Lemon Linguine

SERVES 2

2 small skinless salmon
    fillets, each about 75 g/3 oz
2 tsp sunflower oil
½ tsp mixed or black
    peppercorns, crushed
175 g/6 oz linguine
1 tbsp unsalted butter

4 spring onions, trimmed
    and shredded
150 ml/¼ pint soured cream
finely grated zest of ½ lemon
4–6 tbsp freshly grated
    Parmesan cheese
1 tbsp lemon juice

pinch salt

To garnish:
dill sprigs
lemon slices

Brush the salmon fillets with the sunflower oil, sprinkle with crushed peppercorns and press on firmly and reserve.

Bring a large pan of lightly salted water to a rolling boil. Add the linguine and cook according to the packet instructions, or until *al dente*.

Meanwhile, melt the butter in a saucepan and cook the shredded spring onions gently for 2–3 minutes, or until soft. Stir in the soured cream and the grated lemon zest and remove from the heat.

Preheat a griddle or heavy-based frying pan until very hot. Add the salmon and sear for 1½–2 minutes on each side. Remove from the pan and allow to cool slightly.

Bring the soured cream sauce to the boil and stir in the Parmesan cheese and lemon juice. Drain the pasta thoroughly and return to the pan. Pour over the sauce and toss gently to coat.

Spoon the pasta onto warmed serving plates and top with the salmon fillets.

Serve immediately with sprigs of dill and lemon slices.

Sea Bass in Creamy Watercress & Prosciutto Sauce

SERVES 2

50 g/2 oz watercress
250 ml/8 fl oz fish or
   chicken stock
150 ml/¼ pint dry white wine,
   or use all stock

125 g/4 oz tagliatelle pasta
2 tbsp butter
40 g/1½ oz prosciutto ham
1 tbsp plain flour
150 ml/¼ pint single cream

salt and freshly ground
   black pepper
olive oil, for spraying
2 x 175 g/6 oz sea bass fillets
fresh watercress, to garnish

Remove the leaves from the watercress stalks and reserve. Chop the stalks roughly and put in a large pan with the stock. Bring to the boil slowly, cover and simmer for 20 minutes. Strain and discard the stalks. Make the stock up to 300 ml/½ pint with the wine.

Bring a large saucepan of lightly salted water to the boil and cook the pasta for 8–10 minutes, or until *al dente*. Drain and reserve.

Melt the butter in a saucepan and cook the prosciutto gently for 3 minutes. Remove with a slotted spoon. Stir the flour into the saucepan and cook on a medium heat for 2 minutes. Remove from the heat and gradually pour in the hot watercress stock, stirring continuously. Return to the heat and bring to the boil, stirring throughout. Simmer for 3 minutes, or until the sauce has thickened and is smooth. Purée the watercress leaves and cream in a food processor, then add to the sauce with the prosciutto. Season to taste with salt and pepper, add the pasta, toss lightly and keep warm.

Meanwhile, spray a griddle pan lightly with olive oil, then heat until hot. When hot, cook the fillets for 3–4 minutes on each side, or until cooked. Arrange the sea bass on a bed of pasta and drizzle with a little sauce. Garnish with watercress and serve immediately.

Grilled Red Mullet with Orange & Anchovy Sauce

SERVES 2

2 oranges
2 x 175 g/6 oz red mullet, cleaned and scales removed
salt and freshly ground black pepper

2 fresh rosemary sprigs
½ lemon, sliced
1 tbsp olive oil
2 garlic cloves, peeled and crushed
4 anchovy fillets in oil,

drained and roughly chopped
1 tsp freshly chopped rosemary
1 tsp lemon juice

Preheat the grill and line the grill rack with kitchen foil just before cooking. Peel the oranges with a sharp knife over a bowl in order to catch the juice. Cut into thin slices and reserve.

Place the fish on a chopping board and make 2 diagonal slashes across the thickest part of both sides of the fish. Season well, both inside and out, with salt and pepper. Tuck a rosemary sprig and 1–2 lemon slices inside the cavity of each fish. Brush the fish with a little of the olive oil and then cook under the preheated grill for 4–5 minutes on each side. The flesh should just fall away from the bone.

Heat the remaining oil in a saucepan and gently fry the garlic and anchovies for 3–4 minutes. Do not allow to brown. Add the chopped rosemary and plenty of black pepper. The anchovies will be salty enough, so do not add any salt. Stir in the orange slices with their juice and the lemon juice. Simmer gently until heated through. Spoon the sauce over the red mullet and serve immediately.

Grilled Snapper
with Roasted Peppers

SERVES 2

1 small red pepper
1 small green pepper
2–4 snapper fillets,
    depending on size, about
    450 g/1 lb

sea salt and freshly ground
    black pepper
1–2 tsp olive oil
3 tbsp double cream
85 ml/3 fl oz white wine

1–2 tsp freshly chopped dill
fresh dill sprigs, to garnish
freshly cooked tagliatelle,
    to serve

Preheat the grill to a high heat and line the grill rack with kitchen foil. Cut the tops off the peppers and divide into quarters. Remove the seeds and the membrane, then place on the foil-lined grill rack and cook for 8–10 minutes, turning frequently, until the skins have become charred and blackened. Remove from the grill rack, place in a polythene bag and leave until cool. When the peppers are cool, strip off the skin, slice thinly and reserve.

Cover the grill rack with another piece of kitchen foil, then place the snapper fillets skin-side up on the grill rack. Season to taste with salt and pepper and brush with a little of the olive oil. Cook for 10–12 minutes, turning over once and brushing again with a little olive oil.

Pour the cream and wine into a small saucepan, bring to the boil and simmer for about 5 minutes until the sauce has thickened slightly. Add the dill, season to taste and stir in the sliced peppers. Arrange the cooked snapper fillets on warm serving plates and pour over the cream and pepper sauce. Garnish with sprigs of dill and serve immediately with freshly cooked tagliatelle.

Ratatouille Mackerel

SERVES 2

1 small red pepper
1 small red onion, peeled
1 tbsp olive oil
1 garlic clove, peeled and
   thinly sliced
1 small courgette, trimmed
   and cut into thick slices

200 g/7 oz canned chopped
   tomatoes
sea salt and freshly ground
   black pepper
2 x 300 g/10 oz small
   mackerel, cleaned and
   heads removed

spray of olive oil
lemon juice for drizzling
few fresh basil leaves
couscous or rice mixed with
   chopped parsley, to serve

Preheat the oven to 190°C/375°F/Gas Mark 5. Cut the top off the red pepper, remove the seeds and membrane, then cut into chunks. Cut the red onion into thick wedges.

Heat the oil in a large pan and cook the onion and garlic for 5 minutes or until beginning to soften.

Add the pepper chunks and courgette slices and cook for a further 5 minutes.

Pour in the chopped tomatoes with their juice and cook for a further 5 minutes. Season to taste with salt and pepper and pour into an ovenproof dish.

Season the fish with salt and pepper and arrange on top of the vegetables. Spray with a little olive oil and lemon juice. Cover and cook in the preheated oven for 20 minutes.

Remove the cover, add the basil leaves and return to the oven for a further 5 minutes. Serve immediately with couscous or rice mixed with parsley.

HELPFUL HINT

If you do not want to open a can of chopped tomatoes for just two people, chop 2 medium-sized tomatoes and use them together with 1 teaspoon tomato purée and 2 tablespoons water.

Sweet-&-Sour Fish

SERVES 2

75 g/3 oz carrot, peeled and cut into julienne strips
125 g/4 oz red or green pepper
50 g/2 oz mangetout, cut in half diagonally
75 g/3 oz frozen peas, thawed
2–3 spring onions, trimmed and sliced diagonally into 5 cm/2 inch pieces
225 g/8 oz small thin plaice

fillets, skinned
1 tbsp cornflour
vegetable oil, for frying
sprigs of fresh coriander, to garnish

For the sweet-&-sour sauce:
2 tsp cornflour
250 ml/8 fl oz fish or chicken stock
1 cm/½ inch piece fresh root

ginger, peeled and finely sliced
1 tbsp soy sauce
1 tbsp rice wine vinegar or dry sherry
1 tbsp tomato ketchup or tomato concentrate
1 tbsp Chinese rice vinegar or cider vinegar
1 tbsp soft light brown sugar

Make the sauce. Place the cornflour in a saucepan and gradually whisk in the stock. Stir in the remaining sauce ingredients and bring to the boil, stirring, until the sauce thickens. Simmer for 2 minutes, then remove from the heat and reserve.

Bring a saucepan of water to the boil. Add the carrot, return to the boil and cook for 3 minutes. Add the pepper and cook for 1 minute. Add the mangetout and peas and cook for 30 seconds. Drain and rinse under cold running water, then add to the sauce with the spring onions.

Using a sharp knife, make crisscross slashes across the top of each fish fillet then lightly coat on both sides with the cornflour. Pour enough oil into a large wok to come 5 cm/2 inches up the side. Heat to 190°C/375°F, or until a cube of bread browns in 30 seconds. Fry the fish fillets, 2 at a time, for 3–5 minutes, or until crisp and golden, turning once. Using a fish slice, remove and drain on kitchen paper. Keep warm.

Bring the sauce to the boil, stirring constantly. Arrange the fish on a warmed platter and pour over the hot sauce. Garnish with coriander sprigs and serve immediately.

Trout with Cream Sauce

SERVES 2

300 g/10 oz rainbow trout
fillets, cut into pieces
salt and freshly ground
black pepper
1 tbsp plain white flour
1 tbsp finely chopped dill
groundnut oil, for frying

For the cream sauce:
25 g/1 oz butter
1 bunch spring onions,
trimmed and thickly sliced
1 garlic clove, peeled and
finely chopped
150 ml/¼ pint dry white wine
4 tbsp double cream

1 medium tomato, skinned,
deseeded and cut into
wedges
1 tbsp freshly chopped basil
freshly snipped basil,
to garnish
freshly cooked creamed
herb potatoes, to serve

Remove as many of the tiny pin bones as possible from the trout fillets (lay the fish on a clean chopping board and run your fingers from the tail end of the fish up to the head end – use a pair of tweezers to remove any bones that you can feel), rinse lightly and pat dry on absorbent kitchen paper. Season the flour and stir in the chopped dill, then use to coat the trout fillets.

Pour sufficient oil into a large wok to a depth of 2.5 cm/1 inch deep. Heat until hot and cook the trout for about 3–4 minutes, turning occasionally, or until cooked. Using a slotted spoon, remove and drain on absorbent kitchen paper and keep warm. Drain the wok and wipe clean.

Melt half the butter in the wok, then stir-fry the spring onions and garlic for 2 minutes. Add the wine, bring to the boil and boil rapidly until reduced by half. Stir in the cream with the tomatoes and basil and bring to the boil. Simmer for 1 minute, then add seasoning to taste.

Add the trout to the sauce and heat through until piping hot. Garnish with freshly snipped basil and serve immediately on a bed of creamed herb potatoes.

Foil–baked Fish

SERVES 2

For the tomato sauce:
50 ml/2 fl oz olive oil
2 garlic cloves, peeled and finely chopped
2 shallots, peeled and finely chopped
200 g/7 oz canned chopped Italian tomatoes
1 tbsp freshly chopped

flat-leaf parsley
1½ tbsp basil leaves
salt and freshly ground black pepper

For the fish:
225 g/8 oz red mullet, bass or haddock fillets
225 g/8 oz live mussels

2 squid
4 large raw prawns
1 tbsp olive oil
3 tbsp dry white wine
1 tbsp freshly chopped basil leaves
lemon wedges, to garnish

Preheat oven to 180°C/350°F/Gas Mark 4, 10 minutes before cooking. Heat the oil and gently fry the garlic and shallots for 2 minutes. Stir in the tomatoes and simmer for 10 minutes, breaking the tomatoes down with the wooden spoon. Add the parsley and basil, season to taste with salt and pepper and cook for a further 2 minutes. Reserve and keep warm.

Lightly rinse the fish fillets and cut into portions. Scrub the mussels thoroughly, removing the beard and any barnacles. Discard any mussels that are open. Clean the squid and cut into rings. Peel the prawns and remove the thin black intestinal vein that runs down the back.

HELPFUL HINT

Make a large batch of the sauce and serve it with pasta. Keep covered in the refrigerator until needed, or freeze for up to 1 month. Thaw completely and reheat gently before using.

Cut 2 large pieces of kitchen foil, then place them on a large baking sheet and brush with olive oil. Place 1 fish portion in the centre of each piece of foil. Close the foil to form parcels and bake in the preheated oven for 10 minutes, then remove.

Carefully open up the parcels and add the mussels, squid and prawns. Pour in the wine and spoon over a little of the tomato sauce. Sprinkle with the basil leaves, return to the oven and bake for 5 minutes, or until cooked thoroughly. Discard any unopened mussels, then garnish with lemon wedges and serve with the extra tomato sauce.

Tuna & Mushroom Ragout

SERVES 2

125 g/4 oz basmati and wild rice
25 g/1 oz butter
1 tbsp olive oil
1 small onion, peeled and finely chopped
1 garlic clove, peeled and crushed
150 g/5 oz baby button mushrooms, wiped and halved
1 tbsp plain flour
200 g/7 oz canned chopped tomatoes
1 tbsp freshly chopped parsley
dash of Worcestershire sauce
200 g can tuna in oil, drained

salt and freshly ground black pepper
2 tbsp Parmesan cheese, grated
1 tbsp freshly shredded basil

To serve:
green salad
garlic bread

Cook the basmati and wild rice in a saucepan of boiling salted water for 20 minutes, then drain and return to the pan. Stir in half of the butter, cover the pan and leave to stand for 2 minutes until all of the butter has melted.

Heat the oil and the remaining butter in a frying pan and cook the onion for 1–2 minutes until soft. Add the garlic and mushrooms and continue to cook for a further 3 minutes.

Stir in the flour and cook for 1 minute, then add the tomatoes and bring the sauce to the boil. Add the parsley, Worcestershire sauce and tuna and simmer gently for 3 minutes. Season to taste with salt and freshly ground pepper.

Stir the rice well, then spoon onto 2 warm serving plates and top with the tuna and mushroom mixture. Sprinkle with a spoonful of grated Parmesan cheese and some shredded basil for each portion and serve immediately with a green salad and chunks of garlic bread.

Fresh Tuna Salad

125 g/4 oz mixed salad leaves
125 g/4 oz baby cherry
    tomatoes, halved
    lengthways
50 g/2 oz rocket leaves,
    washed
2 tbsp groundnut oil

300 g/10 oz boned tuna
    steaks, each cut into
    4 small pieces
25 g/1 oz piece fresh
    Parmesan cheese

For the dressing:
4 tbsp olive oil
grated zest and juice of
    1 small lemon
1 tbsp wholegrain mustard
salt and freshly ground
    black pepper

Wash the salad leaves and place in a large salad bowl with the cherry tomatoes and rocket and reserve.

Heat the wok, then add the oil and heat until almost smoking. Add the tuna, skin-side down, and cook for 4–6 minutes, turning once during cooking, or until cooked and the flesh flakes easily. Remove from the heat and leave to stand in the juices for 2 minutes before removing.

Meanwhile, make the dressing. Place the olive oil, lemon zest and juice and mustard in a small bowl or screw-top jar and whisk or shake well until well blended. Season to taste with salt and pepper.

Transfer the tuna to a clean chopping board and flake, then add it to the salad and toss lightly.

Using a swivel blade vegetable peeler, peel the piece of Parmesan cheese into shavings. Divide the salad between 2 large serving plates, drizzle the dressing over the salad, then scatter with the Parmesan shavings.

Seared Tuna with Italian Salsa

SERVES 2

2 x 175 g/6 oz tuna or
    swordfish steaks
salt and freshly ground
    black pepper
2 tbsp Pernod
2 tbsp olive oil
finely grated zest and
    juice of 1 lemon
1 tsp fresh thyme leaves
1 tsp fennel seeds,

lightly roasted
2 sun-dried tomatoes,
    chopped
½–1 tsp dried chilli flakes
assorted salad leaves,
    to serve

For the salsa:
1 small white onion, peeled
    and finely chopped

1 tomato, deseeded
    and sliced
1 tbsp freshly shredded
    basil leaves
1 red chilli, deseeded and
    finely sliced
1½ tbsp extra-virgin olive oil
1 tsp balsamic vinegar
1 tsp, or to taste,
    caster sugar

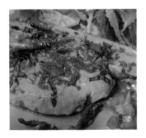

Wipe the fish and season lightly with salt and pepper, then place in a shallow dish. Mix together the Pernod, olive oil, lemon zest and juice, thyme, fennel seeds, sun-dried tomatoes and chilli flakes and pour over the fish. Cover lightly and leave to marinate in a cool place for 1–2 hours, occasionally spooning the marinade over the fish.

Meanwhile, mix all the ingredients for the salsa together in a small bowl. Season to taste with salt and pepper, then cover and leave for about 30 minutes to allow all the flavours to develop.

HELPFUL HINT

If tightly covered and stored in the refrigerator, this salsa should last for five days.

Lightly oil a griddle pan and heat until hot. When the pan is very hot, drain the fish, reserving the marinade. Cook the fish for 3–4 minutes on each side, taking care not to overcook them – the tuna steaks should be a little pink inside. Pour any remaining marinade into a small saucepan, bring to the boil and boil for 1 minute. Serve the steaks hot with the marinade, chilled salsa and a few assorted salad leaves.

Warm Swordfish Niçoise

2 swordfish steaks, about 2.5 cm/1 inch thick, weighing about 175 g/6 oz each
juice of ½ lime
2 tbsp olive oil
salt and freshly ground black pepper

175 g/6 oz farfalle
125 g/4 oz French beans, topped and cut in half
1 tsp Dijon mustard
2 tsp white wine vinegar
pinch caster sugar
1 tbsp olive oil

125 g/4 oz ripe tomatoes, quartered
25 g/1 oz pitted black olives
1 medium egg, hard boiled and quartered
4 anchovy fillets, drained and cut in half lengthways

Place the swordfish steaks in a shallow dish. Mix the lime juice with the oil, season to taste with salt and pepper and spoon over the steaks. Turn the steaks to coat them evenly. Cover and place in the refrigerator to marinate for 1 hour.

Bring a large pan of lightly salted water to a rolling boil. Add the farfalle and cook according to the packet instructions, or until *al dente*. Add the French beans about 4 minutes before the end of cooking time.

Mix the mustard, vinegar and sugar together in a small jug. Gradually whisk in the olive oil to make a thick dressing.

Cook the swordfish in a griddle pan or under a hot preheated grill for 2 minutes on each side, or until just cooked through; overcooking will make it tough and dry. Remove and cut into 2 cm/¾ inch chunks.

Drain the pasta and beans thoroughly and place in a large bowl. Pour over the dressing and toss to coat. Add the cooked swordfish, tomatoes, olives, hard-boiled eggs and anchovy fillets. Gently toss together, taking care not to break up the eggs. Tip into a warmed serving bowl or divide the pasta between individual plates. Serve immediately.

Coconut Fish Curry

SERVES 2

2 tbsp sunflower oil
1 small onion, peeled and
    very finely chopped
1 small yellow pepper,
    deseeded and finely
    chopped
1 garlic clove, peeled and
    crushed
1 tbsp, or to taste, mild
    curry paste
1 cm/½ inch piece root
    ginger, peeled and grated

1 red chilli, deseeded and
    finely chopped
200 ml/7 fl oz canned
    coconut milk
350 g/12 oz firm white fish,
    e.g. monkfish fillets,
    skinned and cut into
    chunks
125 g/4 oz basmati rice
1 tbsp freshly chopped
    coriander
1 tbsp mango chutney

salt and freshly ground
    black pepper

To garnish:
lime wedges
fresh coriander sprigs

To serve:
Greek yogurt
warm naan bread

Put 1 tablespoon of the oil into a large frying pan and cook the onion, pepper and garlic for 5 minutes, or until soft. Add the remaining oil, curry paste, ginger and chilli and cook for a further minute.

Pour in the coconut milk and bring to the boil, reduce the heat and simmer gently for 5 minutes, stirring occasionally. Add the monkfish to the pan and continue to simmer gently for 5–10 minutes, or until the fish is tender but not overcooked.

Meanwhile, cook the rice in a saucepan of boiling salted water for 15 minutes, or until tender. Drain the rice thoroughly and turn out into a serving dish.

Stir the chopped coriander and chutney gently into the fish curry and season to taste with salt and pepper. Spoon the fish curry over the cooked rice, garnish with lime wedges and coriander sprigs and serve immediately with spoonfuls of Greek yogurt and warm naan bread.

Singapore–style Curry

SERVES 2

75 g/3 oz basmati rice
225 g/ 8 oz large prawns, peeled
1 tbsp vegetable oil
2.5 cm/1 inch piece fresh root ginger, peeled and grated

1 red bird's eye chilli, deseeded and sliced
2 shallots, peeled and cut into thin wedges
1 small red pepper, deseeded and cut into small chunks

1 small courgette, trimmed and cut into chunks
2–4 tbsp sweet chilli sauce
125 g/4 oz ripe tomatoes, peeled and chopped
1 tbsp freshly chopped coriander

Cook the rice in a saucepan of boiling water for 12–15 minutes, or until tender. Drain and keep warm. Clean the prawns, removing the thin black thread if necessary, and reserve. Heat the oil in a large pan or wok, add the ginger and chilli and fry for 1 minute.

Add the shallots and red pepper and stir-fry for 3 minutes. Add the courgette, sweet chilli sauce to taste and chopped tomatoes and simmer for 2 minutes.

Add the prawns and continue to simmer for 5 minutes, or until the prawns have turned pink.

Place a portion of cooked rice in the base of 2 deep serving bowls and spoon over some of the prawn mixture and liquor. Sprinkle each with chopped coriander and serve.

Malaysian Fish Curry

SERVES 2

2 firm fish fillets, such as
salmon, haddock or
pollack, each about 150
g/5 oz in weight
1 tbsp groundnut oil
2 garlic cloves, peeled
and crushed
2.5 cm/1 inch piece fresh

root ginger, peeled
and grated
1 tsp turmeric
1 tsp ground coriander
1 tbsp mild or medium
Madras curry paste,
depending on taste
250 ml/8 fl oz coconut milk

1 tbsp freshly chopped
coriander
lime wedges, to garnish
(optional)
stir-fried Oriental vegetables
and fragrant rice, to serve

Preheat the oven to 180°C/350°F/Gas Mark 4. Lightly rinse the fish fillets and pat dry with absorbent kitchen paper. Place in a lightly oiled ovenproof dish.

Heat the oil in a frying pan, add the garlic and ginger and fry for 2 minutes. Add the turmeric, ground coriander and curry paste and cook for a further 3 minutes, stirring frequently. Take off the heat and gradually stir in the coconut milk. Cool slightly, then pour over the fish.

Cover with lightly buttered foil and cook in the preheated oven for 20 minutes, or until the fish is tender. Sprinkle with chopped coriander, then garnish with lime wedges, if using, and serve with stir-fried vegetables and freshly cooked rice.

Red Prawn Curry

SERVES 2

1 tsp coriander seeds
½ tsp cumin seeds
½ tsp black peppercorns
pinch salt
1–2 dried red chillies, depending on heat tolerance
1 shallot, peeled and chopped
1–2 garlic cloves
1 cm/½ inch piece fresh galangal or root ginger, peeled and chopped

1 kaffir lime leaf or ½ tsp kaffir lime zest
½ tsp red chilli powder
1 tsp shrimp paste
1 lemon grass stalk, outer leaves removed, and thinly sliced
450 ml/¾ pint coconut milk
1 red chilli, deseeded and thinly sliced
1 tbsp Thai fish sauce
2 tsp soft brown sugar
1 small red pepper, deseeded

and thinly sliced
300g/10 oz large peeled tiger prawns
1 fresh kaffir lime leaf, shredded (optional)
1 tbsp fresh mint leaves, shredded
1 tbsp Thai or Italian basil leaves, shredded
freshly cooked Thai fragrant rice, to serve

Using a pestle and mortar or a spice grinder, grind the coriander and cumin seeds, peppercorns and salt to a fine powder. Add the dried chillies one at a time and grind to a fine powder.

Place the shallot, garlic, galangal or ginger, kaffir lime leaf or zest, chilli powder and shrimp paste in a food processor. Add the ground spices and process until a thick paste forms. Scrape down the bowl once or twice, adding a few drops of water if the mixture is too thick and not forming a paste. Stir in the lemon grass.

Transfer the paste to a large wok and cook over a medium heat for 2–3 minutes, or until fragrant. Stir in the coconut milk, bring to the boil, then lower the heat and simmer for about 10 minutes. Add the chilli, fish sauce, sugar and red pepper and simmer for 15 minutes.

Stir in the prawns and cook for 5 minutes, or until the prawns are pink and tender. Stir in the shredded herbs, heat for a further minute and serve immediately with the cooked rice.

Fruits de Mer Stir–fry

SERVES 2

350 g/12 oz mixed fresh
    shellfish, such as tiger
    prawns, squid, scallops
    and mussels
2.5 cm/1 inch piece fresh
    root ginger
2 garlic cloves, peeled
    and crushed

1–2 green chillies, deseeded
    and finely chopped
2 tbsp light soy sauce
1 tbsp groundnut or
    sunflower oil
125 g/4 oz baby sweetcorn,
    rinsed
150 g/5 oz asparagus tips,

trimmed and cut in half
125 g/4 oz mangetout,
    trimmed
2 tbsp plum sauce
2 spring onions, trimmed
    and shredded, to garnish
freshly cooked rice, to serve

Prepare the shellfish. Peel the prawns and, if necessary, remove the thin black veins from the back of the prawns. Lightly rinse the squid rings and clean the scallops, if necessary.

Remove and discard any mussels that are open. Scrub and debeard the remaining mussels, removing any barnacles from the shells. Cover the mussels with cold water until required.

Peel the root ginger and either grate coarsely or shred finely with a sharp knife and place into a small bowl. Add the garlic and chillies to the bowl, pour in the soy sauce and mix well.

Place the mixed shellfish, except the mussels, in a bowl and pour over the marinade. Stir, cover and leave for 15 minutes.

Heat a wok until hot, then add the oil and heat until almost smoking. Add the prepared vegetables, stir-fry for 2 minutes, then stir in the plum sauce.

Add the shellfish and the mussels with the marinade and stir-fry for a further 3–4 minutes, or until the fish is cooked. Discard any mussels that have not opened. Garnish with the spring onions and serve immediately with freshly cooked rice.

Mussels Linguine

1 kg/2.2 lb fresh mussels,
washed and scrubbed
knob butter
1 onion, peeled and finely
chopped
200 ml/7 fl oz medium dry
white wine

For the sauce:
1 tbsp sunflower oil
2–3 baby onions, peeled
and quartered
2 garlic cloves, peeled
and crushed
1 x 400 g/14 oz can chopped

tomatoes
large pinch salt
225 g/8 oz dried linguine
or tagliatelle
2 tbsp freshly chopped
parsley, to garnish

Soak the mussels in plenty of cold water. Leave in the refrigerator until required. When ready
to use, scrub the mussel shells, removing any barnacles or beards. Discard any open mussels.

Melt the butter in a large pan. Add the mussels, onion and wine. Cover with a close-fitting lid and
steam for 5–6 minutes, shaking the pan gently to ensure even cooking. Discard any mussels that
have not opened, then strain and reserve the liquor.

To make the sauce, heat the oil in a medium-sized saucepan and gently fry the quartered
onions and garlic for 3–4 minutes until soft and transparent. Stir in the tomatoes and half the
reserved mussel liquor. Bring to the boil and simmer for 7–10 minutes until the sauce begins
to thicken.

Cook the pasta in boiling salted water for 7 minutes, or until *al dente*. Drain the pasta,
reserving 2 tablespoons of the cooking liquor, then return the pasta and liquor to the pan.

Remove the meat from half the mussel shells. Stir into the sauce along with the remaining
mussels. Pour the hot sauce over the cooked pasta and toss gently. Garnish with the parsley
and serve immediately.

Pan–fried Scallops & Pasta

SERVES 2

8 large scallops, shelled
1 tbsp olive oil
1 garlic clove, peeled
   and crushed
1 tsp freshly chopped thyme
175 g/6 oz penne
2 sun-dried tomatoes in oil,
   drained and thinly sliced

thyme or oregano sprigs,
   to garnish

For the tomato dressing:
2 sun-dried tomatoes in oil,
   drained and chopped
1 tbsp red wine vinegar
2 tsp balsamic vinegar

1 tsp sun-dried tomato paste
1 tsp caster sugar
salt and freshly ground
   black pepper
2 tbsp oil from a jar of
   sun-dried tomatoes
2 tbsp olive oil

Rinse the scallops and pat dry on absorbent kitchen paper. Place in a bowl and add the olive oil, crushed garlic and thyme. Cover and chill in the refrigerator until ready to cook.

Bring a large pan of lightly salted water to a rolling boil. Add the penne and cook according to the packet instructions, or until *al dente*.

Meanwhile, make the dressing. Place the sun-dried tomatoes into a small bowl or glass jar and add the vinegars, tomato paste, sugar, salt and pepper. Whisk well, then pour into a food processor. With the motor running, pour in the sun-dried tomato oil and olive oil in a steady stream to make a thick, smooth dressing.

Preheat a large, dry cast-iron griddle pan over a high heat for about 5 minutes. Lower the heat to medium, then add the scallops to the pan. Cook for 1½ minutes on each side. Remove from the pan.

Drain the pasta thoroughly and return to the pan. Add the sliced sun-dried tomatoes and sufficient dressing to moisten, then toss. Divide between individual serving plates, top each portion with 4 scallops, garnish with fresh thyme or oregano sprigs and serve immediately.

HELPFUL HINT

If you have any of the sun-dried tomato dressing left, store in a screw-top jar in a cool, dark place. It is delicious drizzled over salads.

Meat & Poultry

Leek & Ham Risotto

SERVES 2

1 tbsp olive oil
25 g/1 oz butter
1 small onion, peeled
and finely chopped
2 leeks, trimmed and
thinly sliced

1 tbsp freshly chopped thyme
175 g/6 oz Arborio rice
685 ml/1 pint 3 fl oz
vegetable or chicken
stock, heated
125 g/4 oz cooked ham

75 g/3 oz peas, thawed
if frozen
25 g/1 oz Parmesan cheese,
grated
salt and freshly ground
black pepper

Heat the oil and half the butter together in a large saucepan. Add the onion and leeks and cook over a medium heat for 6–8 minutes, stirring occasionally, until soft and beginning to colour. Stir in the thyme and cook briefly.

Add the rice and stir well. Continue stirring over a medium heat for about 1 minute until the rice is glossy. Add a ladleful or two of the stock and stir well until the stock is absorbed. Continue adding stock, a ladleful at a time and stirring well between additions, until about two-thirds of the stock has been added.

Meanwhile, either chop or finely shred the ham, then add to the saucepan of rice together with the peas. Continue adding ladlefuls of stock, as described in step 2, until the rice is tender and the ham is heated through thoroughly.

Add the remaining butter, sprinkle over the Parmesan cheese and season to taste with salt and pepper. When the butter has melted and the cheese has softened, stir well to incorporate. Taste and adjust the seasoning, then serve immediately.

Pork Goulash & Rice

SERVES 2

450 g/1 lb boneless pork
  rib chops
1 tbsp olive oil
1 onion, peeled and roughly
  chopped
1 small red pepper,
  deseeded and thinly sliced
1 garlic clove, peeled and

crushed
1 tbsp plain flour
1 tsp paprika
200 g/7 oz canned chopped
  tomatoes
150 ml/¼ pint water
salt and freshly ground
  black pepper

150 g/5 oz long-grain
  white rice
250 ml/8 fl oz chicken stock
  or water
fresh flat-leaf parsley sprigs,
  to garnish
2–3 tbsp sour cream,
  to serve

Preheat the oven to 140°C/275°F/Gas Mark 1. Cut the pork into large cubes, about 4 cm/1½ inches square. Heat the oil in a large flameproof casserole and brown the pork in batches over a high heat, transferring the cubes to a plate as they brown.

Over a medium heat, add the onion and pepper and cook for about 5 minutes, stirring regularly, until they begin to brown. Add the garlic and return the meat to the casserole along with any juices on the plate. Sprinkle in the flour and paprika and stir well to soak up the oil and juices. Add the tomatoes with 150 ml/¼ pint of water and then season to taste with salt and pepper. Bring slowly to the boil, cover with a tight-fitting lid and cook in the preheated oven for 1½ hours.

Meanwhile, rinse the rice in several changes of water until the water remains relatively clear. Drain well and put into a saucepan with the chicken stock or water and a little salt. Cover tightly and bring to the boil. Turn the heat down as low as possible and cook for 10 minutes without removing the lid. After 10 minutes, remove from the heat and leave for a further 10 minutes without removing the lid. Fluff with a fork.

When the meat is tender, stir in the sour cream lightly to create a marbled effect, or serve separately. Garnish with parsley and serve immediately with the rice.

Pork Fried Noodles

SERVES 2

75 g/3 oz dried thread egg
noodles
50 g/2 oz broccoli florets
2 tbsp groundnut oil
225 g/8 oz pork tenderloin,
sliced
1 tbsp soy sauce
2 tsp lemon juice
pinch sugar

1 tsp chilli sauce
1 tsp sesame oil
1 cm/½ inch piece fresh root
ginger, peeled and cut
into sticks
1 garlic clove, peeled and
chopped
1 green chilli, deseeded
and sliced

50 g/2 oz mangetout, halved
1 medium egg, lightly beaten
125 g/4 oz canned water
chestnuts, drained
and sliced

To garnish:
radish rose
spring onion tassels

Place the noodles in a bowl and cover with boiling water. Leave to stand for 20 minutes, stirring occasionally, or until tender. Drain and reserve. Meanwhile, blanch the broccoli in a saucepan of lightly salted boiling water for 2 minutes. Drain, refresh under cold running water and reserve.

Heat a large wok or frying pan, add the groundnut oil and heat until just smoking. Add the pork and stir-fry for 5 minutes, or until browned. Using a slotted spoon, remove the pork slices and reserve.

Mix together the soy sauce, lemon juice, sugar, chilli sauce and sesame oil and reserve.

Add the ginger to the wok and stir-fry for 30 seconds. Add the garlic and chilli and stir-fry for 30 seconds. Add the reserved broccoli and stir-fry for 3 minutes. Stir in the mangetout, pork and reserved noodles with the beaten egg and water chestnuts and stir-fry for 5 minutes, or until heated through. Pour over the reserved chilli sauce, toss well and turn into a warmed serving dish. Garnish and serve immediately.

Spicy Pork

SERVES 2

2 tbsp groundnut oil
1 cm/½ inch piece fresh root ginger, peeled and cut into matchsticks
1 garlic clove, peeled and chopped
1 medium carrot, peeled and cut into matchsticks

1 small or 2–3 baby aubergine, trimmed and cubed
300 g/10 oz pork fillet, thickly sliced
300 ml/½ pint coconut milk
1 tbsp Thai red curry paste
2 tbsp Thai fish sauce

1 tsp caster sugar
125 g/4 oz canned bamboo shoots in brine, drained and cut into matchsticks
salt, to taste
lime zest strands, to garnish
freshly cooked rice, to serve

Heat a wok or large frying pan, add 1 tablespoon of the oil and, when hot, add the ginger, garlic, carrot and aubergine and stir-fry for 3 minutes. Using a slotted spoon, transfer to a plate and keep warm. Add the remaining oil to the wok, heat until smoking, then add the pork and stir-fry for 5–8 minutes, or until browned all over. Transfer to a plate and keep warm. Wipe the wok clean.

Pour half the coconut milk into the wok, stir in the red curry paste and bring to the boil. Boil rapidly for 2 minutes until slightly thickened.

Add the fish sauce and sugar to the wok and bring back to the boil. Return the pork and vegetables to the wok with the bamboo shoots. Return to the boil, then simmer for 4 minutes.

Stir in the remaining coconut milk and season to taste with salt. Simmer for 2 minutes, or until heated through. Garnish with lime zest and serve immediately with rice.

Pork with Tofu & Coconut

SERVES 2

40 g/1½ oz unsalted cashew nuts
1 tbsp ground coriander
1 tsp ground cumin
1–2 tsp hot chilli powder
1 cm/½ inch piece fresh root ginger, peeled and chopped
1 tbsp oyster sauce
3 tbsp groundnut oil

300 ml/½ pint coconut milk
75 g/3 oz rice noodles
300 g/10 oz pork tenderloin, thickly sliced
1 red chilli, deseeded and sliced
1 green chilli, deseeded and sliced
4 spring onions, trimmed

and thickly sliced
1 medium tomato, roughly chopped
75 g/3 oz tofu, drained
1 tbsp freshly chopped coriander
1 tbsp freshly chopped mint
salt and freshly ground black pepper

Place the cashew nuts, coriander, cumin, chilli powder, ginger and oyster sauce in a food processor and blend until well ground. Heat a wok or large frying pan, add 2 tablespoons of the oil and, when hot, add the cashew mixture and stir-fry for 1 minute. Stir in the coconut milk, bring to the boil, then simmer for 1 minute. Pour into a small jug and reserve. Wipe the wok clean.

Meanwhile, place the rice noodles in a bowl, cover with boiling water, leave to stand for 5 minutes, then drain thoroughly.

Reheat the wok, add the remaining oil and, when hot, add the pork and stir-fry for 5 minutes, or until browned all over. Add the chillies and spring onions and stir-fry for 2 minutes.

Add the tomato and tofu to the wok with the noodles and coconut mixture and stir-fry for a further 2 minutes, or until heated through, being careful not to break up the tofu. Sprinkle with the chopped coriander and mint, season to taste with salt and pepper and stir. Tip into a warmed serving dish and serve immediately.

Fusilli with Spicy Tomato & Chorizo Sauce with Roasted Peppers

SERVES 2

1 small red pepper,
    deseeded and quartered
1 small yellow pepper,
    deseeded and quartered
2 tbsp olive oil
75 g/3 oz chorizo (outer skin
    removed), roughly chopped

2 garlic cloves, peeled and
    finely chopped
large pinch chilli flakes
350 g/12 oz ripe tomatoes,
    skinned and roughly
    chopped
salt and freshly ground

black pepper
225 g/8 oz fusilli
basil leaves, to garnish
freshly grated Parmesan
    cheese, to serve

Preheat the grill to high. Brush the pepper quarters with 1 tablespoon of the olive oil, then cook under the preheated grill, turning once, for 8–10 minutes, or until the skins have blackened and the flesh is tender. Place the peppers in a plastic bag until cool enough to handle. When cooled, peel the peppers, slice very thinly and reserve.

Heat the remaining oil in a frying pan and add the chorizo. Cook over a medium heat for 3–4 minutes, or until starting to brown. Add the garlic and chilli flakes and cook for a further 2–3 minutes.

Add the tomatoes, season lightly with salt and pepper, then cook gently for about 5 minutes, or until the tomatoes have broken down. Lower the heat and cook for a further 10–15 minutes, or until the sauce has thickened. Add the peppers and heat gently for 1–2 minutes. Adjust the seasoning to taste.

Meanwhile, bring a large pan of lightly salted water to a rolling boil. Add the fusilli and cook according to the packet instructions, or until *al dente*. Drain thoroughly and transfer to a warmed serving dish. Pour over the sauce, sprinkle with basil and serve with Parmesan cheese.

Oven–baked Pork Balls with Peppers

SERVES 2

For the garlic bread:
2–4 garlic cloves, peeled
25–40 g/1–1½ oz butter, softened
1 tbsp freshly chopped parsley
2–3 tsp lemon juice
1 small focaccia loaf

For the pork balls:
225 g/8 oz fresh pork mince
1½ tbsp freshly chopped basil
2 garlic cloves, peeled and chopped
2 sun-dried tomatoes, chopped
salt and freshly ground black pepper
2 tbsp olive oil
1 small red pepper, deseeded and cut into chunks
1 small green pepper, deseeded and cut into chunks
1 small yellow pepper, deseeded and cut into chunks
125 g/4 oz cherry tomatoes
1 tbsp balsamic vinegar

Preheat the oven to 200°C/400°F/Gas Mark 6, 15 minutes before cooking. Crush the garlic, then blend with the softened butter, the parsley and enough lemon juice to give a soft consistency. Shape into a roll, wrap in baking parchment and chill in the refrigerator for at least 30 minutes.

Mix together the pork, basil, 1 chopped garlic clove, sun-dried tomatoes and seasoning until well combined. With damp hands, divide the mixture into 8, roll into balls and reserve.

Spoon the olive oil into a large roasting tin and place in the preheated oven for about 3 minutes until very hot. Remove from the heat and stir in the pork balls, the remaining chopped garlic and peppers. Bake for about 15 minutes. Remove from the oven and stir in the cherry tomatoes and season to taste with plenty of salt and pepper. Bake for about 20 minutes more.

Just before the pork balls are ready, slice the bread, toast lightly and spread with the prepared garlic butter. Remove the pork balls from the oven, stir in the vinegar and serve immediately with the garlic bread.

HELPFUL HINT

Prepare the garlic butter ahead to the end of step 1. Refrigerate for up to 1 week or freeze for up to 2 months.

Gammon with Red Wine Sauce & Pasta

SERVES 2

25 g/1 oz butter
150 ml/¼ pint red wine
4 red onions, peeled
and sliced
4 tbsp orange juice

1 tsp soft brown sugar
225 g/8 oz gammon steak,
trimmed
175 g/6 oz fusilli
freshly ground black pepper

3 tbsp wholegrain mustard
2 tbsp freshly chopped flat-
leaf parsley, plus sprigs
to garnish

Preheat the grill to a medium heat before cooking. Heat the butter with the red wine in a large heavy-based pan. Add the onions, cover with a tight-fitting lid and cook over a very low heat for 30 minutes, or until softened and transparent. Remove the lid from the pan, stir in the orange juice and sugar, then increase the heat and cook for about 10 minutes until the onions are golden.

Cook the gammon steak under the preheated grill, turning at least once, for 4–6 minutes, or until tender. Cut the cooked gammon into bite-sized pieces. Reserve and keep warm.

Meanwhile, bring a large pan of very lightly salted water to a rolling boil. Add the pasta and cook according to the packet instructions, or until *al dente*. Drain the pasta thoroughly, return to the pan, season with a little pepper and keep warm.

Stir the wholegrain mustard and chopped parsley into the onion sauce, then pour over the pasta. Add the gammon pieces to the pan and toss lightly to thoroughly coat the pasta with the sauce. Pile the pasta mixture onto two warmed serving plates. Garnish with sprigs of flat-leaf parsley and serve immediately.

Chilli con Carne with Crispy–skinned Potatoes

SERVES 2

1 tbsp vegetable oil, plus extra for brushing
1 small onion, peeled and finely chopped
1 garlic clove, peeled and finely chopped
1 red chilli, deseeded and finely chopped
225 g/8 oz chuck steak, finely chopped, or lean fresh beef mince
1 tbsp, or to taste, chilli powder
200 g/7 oz canned chopped tomatoes
75 ml/3 fl oz beef stock or water
2 tbsp tomato purée
2 large baking potatoes
200 g/7 oz can red kidney beans, drained and rinsed
coarse salt and freshly ground black pepper

To serve:
ready-made guacamole
sour cream

Preheat the oven to 150°C/300°F/Gas Mark 2. Heat the oil in a large flameproof casserole and add the onion. Cook gently for 10 minutes until soft and lightly browned. Add the garlic and chilli and cook briefly. Increase the heat. Add the chuck steak or lean mince and cook for a further 10 minutes, stirring occasionally, until browned.

Add the chilli powder and stir well. Cook for about 2 minutes, then add the chopped tomatoes, beef stock or water and tomato purée. Bring slowly to the boil. Cover with the lid and place in the oven.

Meanwhile, brush a little vegetable oil all over the potatoes and rub on some coarse salt. Put the potatoes in the oven alongside the chilli. Cook in the preheated oven for 1–1½ hours.

Remove the chilli from the oven and stir in the kidney beans. Return to the oven for a further 15 minutes, or until the potatoes are tender.

Remove the chilli and potatoes from the oven. Cut a cross in each potato, then squeeze to open slightly and season to taste with salt and pepper. Serve with the chilli, guacamole and sour cream.

HELPFUL HINT

Make guacamole by peeling, stoning and mashing 1 large avocado with 2 tablespoons each of lemon juice and crème fraîche, ¼ teaspoon Tabasco sauce, 1 crushed garlic clove and salt and pepper.

Fried Rice with Chilli Beef

SERVES 2

125 g/4 oz beef fillet
175 g/6 oz long-grain rice
3 tbsp groundnut oil
2 onions, peeled and
   thinly sliced

1 hot red chilli, deseeded
   and finely chopped
1 tbsp light soy sauce
1 tsp tomato paste
salt and freshly ground

black pepper
2 tbsp milk
2 tbsp flour
1 tbsp butter
1 large egg

Trim the beef fillet, discarding any fat, then cut into thin strips and reserve. Cook the rice in boiling salted water for 15 minutes, or according to packet instructions, then drain and reserve.

Heat a wok and add 2 tablespoons of oil. When hot, add 1 of the onions and stir-fry for 2–3 minutes. Add the beef to the wok, together with the chilli, and stir-fry for a further 3 minutes, or until tender.

Add the rice to the wok with the soy sauce and tomato paste. Stir-fry for 1–2 minutes, or until piping hot. Season to taste with salt and pepper and keep warm. Meanwhile, toss the remaining onion in the milk, then the flour, in batches. In a small frying pan-fry the onion in the last 1 tablespoon of oil until crisp, then reserve.

Melt the butter in a small omelette pan. Beat the eggs with 2 teaspoons of water and pour into the pan. Cook gently, stirring frequently, until the egg has set, forming an omelette, then slide onto a clean chopping board and cut into thin strips. Add to the fried rice, sprinkle with the crispy onion and serve immediately.

Coconut Beef

SERVES 2

225 g/8 oz beef rump or
  sirloin steak
2 tbsp groundnut oil
1 bunch spring onions,
  trimmed and thickly sliced
1 red chilli, deseeded and
  chopped
1 garlic clove, peeled

and chopped
1 cm/½ inch piece fresh root
  ginger, peeled and cut
  into matchsticks
50 g/2 oz shiitake
  mushrooms, wiped and
  trimmed
100 ml/3½ fl oz coconut

cream
85 ml/3 fl oz chicken stock
1 tbsp freshly chopped
  coriander
salt and freshly ground
  black pepper
freshly cooked rice, to serve

Trim off any fat or gristle from the beef and cut into thin strips. Heat a wok or large frying pan, add 1 tablespoon of the oil and heat until just smoking. Add the beef and cook for 4–5 minutes, turning occasionally, until browned on all sides. Using a slotted spoon, transfer the beef to a plate and keep warm.

Add the remaining oil to the wok and heat until almost smoking. Add the spring onions, chilli, garlic and ginger and cook for 1 minute, stirring occasionally. Add the mushrooms and stir-fry for 3 minutes. Using a slotted spoon, transfer the mushroom mixture to a plate and keep warm.

Return the beef to the wok, pour in the coconut cream and the stock. Bring to the boil and simmer for 3–4 minutes, or until the juices are slightly reduced and the beef is just tender.

Return the mushroom mixture to the wok and heat through. Stir in the chopped coriander and season to taste with salt and pepper. Serve immediately with freshly cooked rice.

Szechuan Beef

225 g/8 oz beef fillet
1 tbsp hoisin sauce
1 tbsp yellow bean sauce
1 tbsp dry sherry
1 tbsp brandy
2 tbsp groundnut oil
1 red chilli, deseeded
    and sliced
4 spring onions, trimmed
    and chopped

1–2 garlic cloves, peeled
    and chopped
1 cm/½ inch piece fresh root
    ginger, peeled and cut
    into matchsticks
1 small carrot, peeled, sliced
    lengthways and cut into
    short lengths
1 small green pepper,
    deseeded and cut into

2.5 cm/1 inch pieces
125 g/4 oz canned water
    chestnuts, drained and
    halved
fresh coriander sprigs,
    to garnish
freshly cooked noodles with
    freshly ground Szechuan
    peppercorns, to serve

Trim the beef, discarding any sinew or fat, then cut into 5 mm/¼ inch strips. Place in a large shallow dish. In a bowl, stir the hoisin sauce, yellow bean sauce, sherry and brandy together until well blended. Pour over the beef and turn until coated evenly. Cover with clingfilm and leave to marinate for at least 30 minutes.

Heat a wok or large frying pan, add the oil and, when hot, add the chilli, spring onions, garlic and ginger and stir-fry for 2 minutes, or until softened. Using a slotted spoon, transfer to a plate and keep warm.

Add the carrot and pepper to the wok and stir-fry for 4 minutes, or until slightly softened. Transfer to a plate and keep warm.

Drain the beef, reserving the marinade, add to the wok and stir-fry for 3–5 minutes, or until browned. Return the chilli mixture, the carrot and pepper mixture and the marinade to the wok, add the water chestnuts and stir-fry for 2 minutes, or until heated through. Garnish with sprigs of coriander and serve immediately with the noodles.

Spaghetti Bolognese

SERVES 2

1 small carrot
1 celery stalk
1 onion
2 garlic cloves
225 g/8 oz fresh lean beef
   steak, minced
125 g/4 oz smoked streaky
   bacon, rind removed,

and chopped
2 tsp plain flour
150 ml/¼ pint red wine
200 g/7 oz canned chopped
   tomatoes
1 tbsp tomato purée
1 tsp dried mixed herbs
salt and freshly ground

black pepper
pinch sugar
175 g/6 oz spaghetti
fresh oregano sprigs,
   to garnish
Parmesan cheese shavings,
   to serve

Peel and chop the carrot, trim and chop the celery, then peel and chop the onion and garlic. Heat a large nonstick frying pan and sauté the beef and bacon for 5–10 minutes, stirring occasionally, until browned. Add the prepared vegetables to the frying pan and cook for about 3 minutes, or until softened, stirring occasionally.

Add the flour and cook for 1 minute. Stir in the red wine, tomatoes, tomato purée, mixed herbs, seasoning to taste and sugar. Bring to the boil, then cover and simmer for 45 minutes, stirring occasionally.

Meanwhile, bring a large saucepan of lightly salted water to the boil and cook the spaghetti for 10–12 minutes, or until *al dente*. Drain well and divide between two serving plates. Spoon over the sauce, garnish with a few sprigs of oregano and serve immediately with plenty of Parmesan shavings.

HELPFUL HINT
Invest in small rigid freezeable containers to freeze any leftovers.

Pan-fried Beef with Creamy Mushrooms

SERVES 2

125 g/4 oz shallots, peeled
2 garlic cloves, peeled
2 tbsp olive oil
2 medallions beef
2 plum tomatoes

125 g/4 oz flat mushrooms
3 tbsp brandy
150 ml/¼ pint red wine
salt and freshly ground
    black pepper

2 tbsp double cream

To serve:
baby new potatoes
freshly cooked green beans

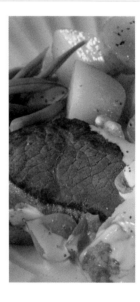

Cut the shallots in half if large, then chop the garlic. Heat the oil in a large frying pan and cook the shallots for about 8 minutes, stirring occasionally, until almost softened. Add the garlic and beef and cook for 4–10 minutes, turning once during cooking, until the meat is browned all over and cooked to personal preference. Using a slotted spoon, transfer the beef to a plate and keep warm.

Rinse the tomatoes and cut into eighths, then wipe the mushrooms and slice. Add to the pan and cook for 5 minutes, stirring frequently, until the mushrooms have softened.

Pour in the brandy and heat through. Draw the pan off the heat and carefully ignite. Allow the flames to subside. Pour in the wine, return to the heat and bring to the boil. Boil until reduced by one third. Draw the pan off the heat, season to taste with salt and pepper, add the cream and stir.

Arrange the beef on serving plates and spoon over the sauce. Serve with baby new potatoes and a few green beans.

HELPFUL HINT

For rare beef steaks, cook for 2 minutes on each side, for medium rare cook for 3 minutes each side and for well done cook for 4–5 minutes each side.

Brandied Lamb Chops

SERVES 2

4 lamb loin chops
2 tbsp groundnut oil
2.5 cm/1 inch piece fresh
    root ginger, peeled and
    cut into matchsticks
2 garlic cloves, peeled
    and chopped
125 g/4 oz button

mushrooms, wiped and
    halved if large
1 tbsp light soy sauce
2 tbsp dry sherry
1 tbsp brandy
1 tsp Chinese five-spice
    powder
1 tsp soft brown sugar

100 ml/3½ fl oz lamb
    or chicken stock
1 tsp sesame oil

To serve:
freshly cooked rice
freshly stir-fried vegetables

Using a sharp knife, trim the lamb chops, discarding any sinew or fat. Heat a wok or large frying pan, add the oil and, when hot, add the lamb chops and cook for 3 minutes on each side, or until browned. Using a fish slice, transfer the lamb chops to a plate and keep warm.

Add the ginger, garlic and button mushrooms to the wok and stir-fry for 3 minutes, or until the mushrooms have browned.

Return the lamb chops to the wok together with the soy sauce, sherry, brandy, five-spice powder and sugar. Pour in the stock, bring to the boil, then reduce the heat slightly and simmer for 4–5 minutes, or until the lamb is tender, ensuring that the liquid does not evaporate completely. Add the sesame oil and heat for a further 30 seconds. Turn into a warmed serving dish and serve immediately with freshly cooked rice and stir-fried vegetables.

Spicy Lamb & Peppers

SERVES 2

300 g/10 oz lamb fillet
2 tbsp soy sauce
1 tbsp dry sherry
1 tbsp cornflour
2 tbsp vegetable oil
4 spring onions, shredded
125 g/4 oz broccoli florets
2 garlic cloves, peeled
   and chopped

1 cm/½ inch piece fresh root
   ginger, peeled and cut
   into matchsticks
1 small red pepper, deseeded
   and cut into chunks
1 small green pepper,
   deseeded and cut
   into chunks
2 tsp Chinese five-spice

   powder
1–2 tsp dried crushed
   chillies, or to taste
1 tbsp tomato purée
1 tbsp rice wine vinegar
1 tbsp soft brown sugar
freshly cooked noodles,
   to serve

Cut the lamb into 2 cm/¾ inch slices, then place in a shallow dish. Blend the soy sauce, sherry and cornflour together in a small bowl and pour over the lamb. Turn the lamb until coated lightly with the marinade. Cover with clingfilm and leave to marinate in the refrigerator for at least 30 minutes, turning occasionally.

Heat a wok or large frying pan, add the oil and, when hot, stir-fry the spring onions and broccoli for 2 minutes. Add the garlic, ginger and peppers and stir-fry for a further 2 minutes. Using a slotted spoon, transfer the vegetables to a plate and keep warm.

Using a slotted spoon, lift the lamb from the marinade, shaking off any excess marinade. Add to the wok and stir-fry for 5 minutes, or until browned all over. Reserve the marinade.

Return the vegetables to the wok and stir in the Chinese five-spice powder, chillies, tomato purée, reserved marinade, vinegar and sugar. Bring to the boil, stirring constantly, until thickened. Simmer for 2 minutes, or until heated through thoroughly. Serve immediately with noodles.

Lamb with Black Cherry Sauce

SERVES 2

300 g/10 oz lamb fillet
1 tbsp light soy sauce
1 tsp Chinese five-spice
   powder
2 tbsp fresh orange juice
75 g/3 oz black cherry jam

150 ml/¼ pint red wine
50 g/2 oz fresh black cherries
1 tbsp groundnut oil

To garnish:
1 tbsp freshly chopped

coriander
whole cherries

To serve:
freshly cooked peas
freshly cooked noodles

Remove the skin and any fat from the lamb fillet and cut into thin slices. Place in a shallow dish. Mix together the soy sauce, Chinese five-spice powder and orange juice and pour over the meat. Cover and leave in the refrigerator for at least 30 minutes.

Meanwhile, blend the jam and the wine together, pour into a small saucepan and bring to the boil. Simmer gently for 10 minutes until slightly thickened. Remove the stones from the fresh cherries, using a cherry stoner if possible in order to keep them whole. Add the cherries to the sauce.

Drain the lamb when ready to cook. Heat the wok, add the oil and, when the oil is hot, stir-fry the slices of lamb for 3–5 minutes, or until just slightly pink inside, or cooked to personal preference.

Spoon the lamb into a warmed serving dish and serve immediately with a little of the cherry sauce drizzled over. Garnish with the chopped coriander and the whole cherries and serve immediately with peas, freshly cooked noodles and the remaining sauce.

Spicy Lamb in Yogurt Sauce

SERVES 2

½–1 tsp hot chilli powder
1 tsp ground cinnamon
½–1 tsp medium hot
    curry powder
½ tsp ground cumin
salt and freshly ground
    black pepper
2 tbsp groundnut oil
250 g/9 oz lamb fillet,
    trimmed

3 cardamom pods, bruised
1 whole clove
1 small onion, peeled and
    finely sliced
2 garlic cloves, peeled
    and crushed
1 cm/½ inch piece fresh root
    ginger, peeled and grated
150 ml/¼ pint Greek-style
    yogurt

1 tbsp freshly chopped
    coriander
2 spring onions, trimmed
    and finely sliced

To serve:
freshly cooked rice
naan bread

Blend the chilli powder, cinnamon, curry powder, cumin and seasoning with 1 tablespoon of the oil in a bowl and reserve. Cut the lamb fillet into thin strips, add to the spice and oil mixture and stir until coated thoroughly. Cover and leave to marinate in the refrigerator for at least 30 minutes.

Heat the wok, then pour in the remaining oil. When hot, add the cardamom pods and clove and stir-fry for 10 seconds. Add the onion, garlic and ginger to the wok and stir-fry for 3–4 minutes until softened.

HELPFUL HINT

Whole spices retain their freshness far longer than ready-ground ones. It is therefore better to buy whole spices in small quantities and grind them in a clean coffee or spice grinder as needed.

Add the lamb with the marinade and stir-fry for a further 3 minutes until cooked. Pour in the yogurt, stir thoroughly and heat until piping hot. Sprinkle with the chopped coriander and sliced spring onions, then serve immediately with freshly cooked rice and naan bread.

Lamb Arrabbiata

SERVES 2

2 tbsp olive oil
300 g/10 oz lamb fillets, trimmed and diced
1 small onion, peeled and sliced
2 garlic cloves, peeled and finely chopped

1 red chilli, deseeded and finely chopped
200 g/7 oz canned chopped tomatoes
75 g/3 oz pitted black olives, halved
150 ml/¼ pint white wine

salt and freshly ground black pepper
175 g/6 oz farfalle pasta
1 tsp butter
2 tbsp freshly chopped parsley, plus 1 tbsp to garnish

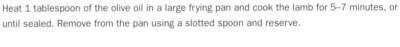

Heat 1 tablespoon of the olive oil in a large frying pan and cook the lamb for 5–7 minutes, or until sealed. Remove from the pan using a slotted spoon and reserve.

Heat the remaining oil in the pan, add the onion, garlic and chilli and cook until softened. Add the tomatoes, bring to the boil, then simmer for 10 minutes, stirring occasionally.

Return the browned lamb to the pan with the olives and pour in the wine. Bring the sauce back to the boil, reduce the heat, then simmer, uncovered, for 15 minutes until the lamb is tender. Season to taste with salt and pepper.

Meanwhile, bring a large pan of lightly salted water to a rolling boil. Add the pasta and cook according to the packet instructions, or until *al dente*.

Drain the pasta, toss in the butter, then add to the sauce and mix lightly. Stir in half the chopped parsley, then tip into a warmed serving dish. Sprinkle with the remaining parsley and serve immediately.

Chicken & Summer Vegetable Risotto

SERVES 2

600 ml/1 pint chicken or
  vegetable stock
125 g/4 oz baby asparagus
  spears
50 g/2 oz French beans
15 g/½ oz butter
1 small onion, peeled and

finely chopped
150 ml/¼ pint dry
  white wine
150 g/5 oz Arborio rice
pinch saffron strands
40 g/1½ oz frozen peas,
  thawed

125 g/4 oz cooked chicken,
  skinned and diced
juice of ½ lemon
salt and freshly ground
  black pepper
15 g/½ oz Parmesan, shaved

Bring the stock to the boil in a large saucepan. Trim the asparagus and cut into 4 cm/1½ inch lengths. Blanch the asparagus in the stock for 1–2 minutes, or until tender, then remove with a slotted spoon and reserve. Halve the green beans and cook in the boiling stock for 4 minutes. Remove and reserve. Turn down the heat and keep the stock barely simmering.

Melt the butter in a heavy-based saucepan. Add the onion and cook gently for about 5 minutes. Pour the wine into the pan and boil rapidly until the liquid has almost reduced. Add the rice and cook, stirring, for 1 minute until the grains are coated and look translucent.

Add the saffron and a ladleful of the stock. Simmer, stirring all the time, until the stock is absorbed. Continue adding the stock, a ladleful at a time, until it has all been absorbed. After 15 minutes, the risotto should be creamy with a slight bite to it. If not, add a little more stock and cook for a few more minutes, or until it is of the correct texture and consistency.

Add the peas, reserved vegetables, chicken and lemon juice. Season to taste with salt and pepper and cook for 3–4 minutes, or until the chicken is thoroughly heated and piping hot. Spoon the risotto on to warmed serving plates. Scatter each portion with Parmesan shavings and serve immediately.

Mexican Chicken

SERVES 2

2 chicken joints, preferably
   off the bone
1 tbsp plain flour
½ tsp ground paprika
salt and freshly ground
   black pepper
2 tsp sunflower oil
1 small onion, peeled
   and chopped
1 red chilli, deseeded and
   finely chopped

½ tsp ground cumin
½ tsp dried oregano
300 ml/½ pint chicken or
   vegetable stock
1 small green pepper,
   deseeded and sliced
2 tsp cocoa powder
1 tbsp lime juice
2 tsp clear honey
3 tbsp Greek yogurt

To garnish:
sliced limes
red chilli slices
fresh oregano sprigs

To serve:
freshly cooked rice
fresh green salad leaves

Using a knife, remove the skin from the chicken joints. In a shallow dish, mix together the flour, paprika, salt and pepper. Coat the chicken on both sides with flour and shake off any excess, if necessary.

Heat the oil in a large nonstick frying pan. Add the chicken and brown on both sides. Transfer to a plate and reserve. Add the onion and chilli to the pan and cook gently for 5 minutes, or until the onion is soft. Stir occasionally. Stir in the cumin and oregano and cook for a further minute. Pour in the stock and bring to the boil. Return the chicken to the pan, cover and cook for 25 minutes. Add the pepper and cook for 10 minutes, until the chicken is cooked. Remove the chicken and pepper with a slotted spoon and keep warm in a serving dish.

Blend the cocoa powder with 1 tablespoon warm water. Stir into the sauce, then boil rapidly until the sauce has thickened and reduced by about one third. Stir in the lime juice, honey and yogurt. Pour the sauce over the chicken and pepper and garnish with the lime slices, chilli and oregano. Serve immediately with the freshly cooked rice and green salad.

Pad Thai

125 g/4 oz flat rice noodles
1 tbsp vegetable oil
125 g/4 oz boneless chicken breast, skinned and thinly sliced
2 shallots, peeled and thinly sliced
2 garlic cloves, peeled and finely chopped
4 spring onions, trimmed and diagonally cut into

5 cm/2 inch pieces
175 g/6 oz fresh white crab meat or tiny prawns
40 g/1½ oz fresh beansprouts, rinsed and drained
1 tbsp preserved or fresh radish, chopped
2 tbsp roasted peanuts, chopped (optional)

For the sauce:
1½ tbsp Thai fish sauce (nam pla)
1-2 tbsp rice vinegar or cider vinegar
2 tsp chilli bean or oyster sauce
1 tsp toasted sesame oil
1-2 tsp light brown sugar
1 red chilli, deseeded and thinly sliced

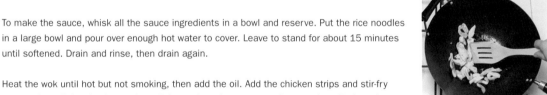

To make the sauce, whisk all the sauce ingredients in a bowl and reserve. Put the rice noodles in a large bowl and pour over enough hot water to cover. Leave to stand for about 15 minutes until softened. Drain and rinse, then drain again.

Heat the wok until hot but not smoking, then add the oil. Add the chicken strips and stir-fry constantly until they begin to colour. Using a slotted spoon, transfer to a plate. Reduce the heat to medium-high. Add the shallots, garlic and spring onions and stir-fry for 1 minute. Stir in the rice noodles, then the reserved sauce; mix well.

Add the reserved chicken strips, with the crab meat or prawns, beansprouts and radish and stir well. Cook for about 5 minutes, stirring frequently, until heated through. If the noodles begin to stick, add a little water.

Turn into a large shallow serving dish and sprinkle with the chopped peanuts, if desired. Serve immediately.

Parma Ham–wrapped Chicken with Ribbon Pasta

SERVES 2

2 boneless, skinless chicken
   breasts
salt and freshly ground
   black pepper
6 slices Parma ham
1 tbsp olive oil
175 g/6 oz ribbon pasta

1 garlic clove, peeled and
   chopped
3 spring onions, trimmed
   and diagonally sliced
200 g/7 oz canned chopped
   tomatoes
juice of 1 lemon

3–4 tbsp crème fraîche
1 tbsp freshly chopped
   parsley
pinch sugar
freshly grated Parmesan
   cheese, to garnish

Cut each chicken breast into 3 pieces and season well with salt and pepper. Wrap each chicken piece in a slice of Parma ham to enclose completely, securing, if necessary, with either fine twine or cocktail sticks.

Heat the oil in a large frying pan and cook the chicken, turning occasionally, for 12–15 minutes, or until thoroughly cooked. Remove from the pan with a slotted spoon and reserve.

Meanwhile, bring a large pan of lightly salted water to a rolling boil. Add the pasta and cook according to the packet instructions, or until *al dente*.

Add the garlic and spring onions to the frying pan and cook, stirring occasionally, for 2 minutes, or until softened. Stir in the tomatoes, lemon juice and crème fraîche. Bring to the boil, lower the heat and simmer, covered, for 3 minutes. Stir in the parsley and sugar, season to taste, then return the chicken to the pan and heat for 2–3 minutes, or until piping hot. Drain the pasta thoroughly and mix in the chopped parsley, then spoon onto a warmed serving dish or individual plates. Arrange the chicken and sauce over the pasta. Garnish with the Parmesan cheese and serve immediately.

Chicken & New Potatoes on Rosemary Skewers

SERVES 2

4–6 thick fresh rosemary stems, at least 23 cm/9 inches long
1–2 tbsp extra-virgin olive oil
2 garlic cloves, peeled and crushed
1 tsp freshly chopped thyme

finely grated zest and juice of 1 lemon
salt and freshly ground black pepper
2 skinless chicken breast fillets
8 small new potatoes, peeled or scrubbed

4 tiny baby onions or shallots, peeled
1 small yellow or red pepper, deseeded
lemon wedges, to garnish
parsley-flavoured cooked rice, to serve

Preheat the grill and line the grill rack with kitchen foil just before cooking. If using a barbecue, light at least 20 minutes before required. Strip the leaves from the rosemary stems, leaving about 5 cm/2 inches of soft leaves at the top. Chop the leaves coarsely and reserve. Using a sharp knife, cut the thicker woody ends of the stems to a point which can pierce the chicken pieces and potatoes. Blend the chopped rosemary, oil, garlic, thyme and lemon zest and juice in a shallow dish. Season to taste with salt and pepper.

Cut the chicken into 4 cm/1½ inch cubes, add to the flavoured oil and stir well. Cover and refrigerate for at least 30 minutes, turning occasionally.

Cook the potatoes in lightly salted boiling water for 10–12 minutes until just tender. Add the onions to the potatoes 2 minutes before the end of the cooking time. Drain, rinse under cold running water and leave to cool. Cut the pepper into 2.5 cm/1 inch squares.

Beginning with a piece of chicken, alternately thread equal amounts of chicken, potato, pepper and onion onto each skewer. Cover the leafy ends with foil to stop them from burning. Do not thread the chicken and vegetables too closely together or the chicken may not cook completely. Cook the kebabs for 15 minutes, or until tender and golden, turning and brushing with either extra oil or the marinade. Remove the foil, garnish with lemon wedges and serve on rice.

Warm Chicken & Potato Salad with Peas & Mint

SERVES 2

225 g/8 oz new potatoes, peeled or scrubbed and cut into bite-sized pieces
salt and freshly ground black pepper
1 tbsp raspberry or cider vinegar
75 g/3 oz frozen garden peas, thawed
1 small ripe avocado
2 cooked chicken breasts, about 450 g/1 lb in weight, skinned and diced
1 tbsp freshly chopped mint
1 head little gem lettuce
fresh mint sprigs, to garnish

For the dressing:
1½ tbsp raspberry or sherry vinegar
1 tsp Dijon mustard
1 tsp clear honey
25 ml/1 fl oz sunflower oil
50 ml/2 fl oz extra-virgin olive oil

Cook the potatoes in lightly salted boiling water for 15 minutes, or until just tender when pierced with the tip of a sharp knife; do not overcook. Rinse under cold running water to cool slightly, then drain and turn into a large bowl. Sprinkle with the raspberry or cider vinegar and toss gently.

Run the peas under hot water to ensure that they are thawed, pat dry with absorbent kitchen paper and add to the potatoes.

Cut the avocado in half lengthways and remove the stone. Peel and cut the avocado into cubes and add to the potatoes and peas. Add the chicken and stir together lightly.

To make the dressing, place all the ingredients in a screw-top jar with a little salt and pepper and shake well to mix; add a little more oil if the flavour is too sharp. Pour over the salad and toss gently to coat. Sprinkle in half the mint and stir lightly.

Separate the lettuce leaves and spread onto a large shallow serving plate. Spoon the salad on top and sprinkle with the remaining mint. Garnish with mint sprigs and serve.

Grilled Spiced Chicken with Tomato & Shallot Chutney

SERVES 2

2 tbsp sunflower oil
1 hot red chilli, deseeded
  and chopped
2 garlic cloves, peeled
  and chopped
2 tsp ground turmeric
½ tsp cumin seeds
1 tsp fennel seeds
2 tsp freshly chopped basil
1–2 tsp dark brown sugar

50 ml/2 fl oz rice or white
  wine vinegar
1 tsp sesame oil
2 large chicken breast
  quarters, wings attached
125 g/4 oz small shallots,
  peeled and halved
1 tbsp Chinese rice wine or
  dry sherry
25 g/1 oz caster sugar

75 g/3 oz cherry tomatoes,
  halved
1 tbsp light soy sauce

To garnish:
fresh coriander sprigs
fresh dill sprigs
lemon wedges

Preheat the grill to medium, 5 minutes before cooking. Heat a wok or large frying pan, add 1 tablespoon of the sunflower oil and, when hot, add the chilli, half the garlic, turmeric, cumin, fennel seeds and basil. Fry for 5 minutes, add the sugar and 1 tablespoon of vinegar and stir until the sugar has dissolved. Remove from the heat, stir in the sesame oil and leave to cool.

Cut 3 or 4 deep slashes in the thickest part of the chicken breasts. Spread the spice paste over the chicken, place in a dish, cover and marinate in the refrigerator for at least 4 hours or overnight.

Heat the remaining sunflower oil in a saucepan, add the shallots and remaining garlic and cook gently for 15 minutes. Add the remaining vinegar, Chinese rice wine or sherry and caster sugar with 50 ml/2 fl oz water. Bring to the boil and simmer rapidly for 10 minutes, or until thickened. Add the tomatoes with the soy sauce. Simmer for 5–10 minutes, or until reduced. Leave to cool.

Transfer the chicken pieces to a grill pan and cook under the preheated grill for 15–20 minutes on each side, or until the chicken is cooked through, basting frequently. Garnish with coriander sprigs and lemon wedges and serve immediately with the chutney.

Aromatic Chicken Curry

SERVES 2

50 g/2 oz red lentils
1 tsp ground coriander
½ tsp cumin seeds
1–2 tsp mild curry paste
1 bay leaf
small strip lemon zest
450 ml/¾ pint chicken or

vegetable stock
4 chicken thighs, skinned
75 g/3 oz spinach leaves,
  rinsed and shredded
1 tbsp freshly chopped
  coriander
2 tsp lemon juice

salt and freshly ground
  black pepper

To serve:
freshly cooked rice
natural yogurt

Put the lentils in a sieve and rinse thoroughly under cold running water.

Dry-fry the ground coriander and cumin seeds in a large saucepan over a low heat for about 30 seconds. Stir in the curry paste. Add the lentils to the saucepan with the bay leaf and lemon zest, then pour in the stock.

Stir, then slowly bring to the boil. Turn down the heat, half-cover the pan with a lid and simmer gently for 5 minutes, stirring occasionally.

Secure the chicken thighs with cocktail sticks to keep their shape. Place in the pan and half-cover. Simmer for 15 minutes.

Stir in the shredded spinach and cook for a further 25 minutes, or until the chicken is very tender and the sauce is thick.

Remove the bay leaf and lemon zest. Stir in the coriander and lemon juice, then season to taste with salt and pepper. Serve immediately with the rice and a little natural yogurt.

Chicken Tikka Masala

2 skinless chicken breast
   fillets
85 ml/3 fl oz natural yogurt
1 garlic clove, peeled and
   crushed
1 cm/½ inch piece fresh root
   ginger, peeled
   and grated
1 tsp chilli powder

2 tsp ground coriander
1–2 tbsp lime juice
twist of lime, to garnish
freshly cooked rice, to serve

For the masala sauce:
1 tbsp unsalted butter
1 tbsp sunflower oil
1 small onion, peeled

   and chopped
1 green chilli, deseeded and
   finely chopped
1 tsp garam masala
85 ml/3 fl oz double cream
salt and freshly ground
   black pepper
1 tbsp fresh coriander
   leaves, roughly torn

Preheat the oven to 200°C/400°F/Gas Mark 6, 15 minutes before cooking. Cut each chicken breast across into 3 pieces, then make 2 or 3 shallow cuts in each piece. Put in a shallow dish. Mix together the yogurt, garlic, ginger, chilli powder, ground coriander and lime juice. Pour over the chicken, cover and marinate in the refrigerator for up to 24 hours.

Remove the chicken from the marinade and arrange on an oiled baking tray. Bake in the preheated oven for 15 minutes, or until golden brown and cooked.

While the chicken is cooking, heat the butter and oil in a wok and stir-fry the onion for 5 minutes, or until tender. Add the chilli and garam masala and stir-fry for a few more seconds. Stir in the cream and remaining marinade. Simmer over a low heat for 1 minute, stirring all the time.

Add the chicken pieces and cook for a further 1 minute, stirring to coat in the sauce. Season to taste with salt and pepper. Transfer the chicken pieces to a warmed serving plate. Stir the torn coriander into the sauce, then spoon over the chicken, garnish with the lime and serve immediately with freshly cooked rice.

Thai Chicken with Chilli & Peanuts

SERVES 2

2 tbsp vegetable or
    groundnut oil
1 garlic clove, peeled and
    finely chopped
1 tsp dried chilli flakes
225 g/8 oz boneless, skinless
    chicken breast, finely sliced

1 tbsp Thai fish sauce
2 tbsp peanuts, roasted and
    roughly chopped
125 g/4 oz sugar snap peas
2 tbsp chicken stock
1 tbsp light soy sauce
1 tbsp dark soy sauce

large pinch sugar
freshly chopped coriander,
    to garnish
boiled or steamed rice,
    to serve

Heat a wok or large frying pan, add the oil and, when hot, carefully swirl the oil around the wok until the sides are lightly coated with the oil. Add the garlic and stir-fry for 10–20 seconds, or until starting to brown. Add the chilli flakes and stir-fry for a few more seconds.

Add the finely sliced chicken to the wok and stir-fry for 2–3 minutes, or until the chicken has turned white.

Add the following ingredients, stirring well after each addition: fish sauce, peanuts, sugar snap peas, chicken stock, light and dark soy sauces and sugar. Give a final stir.

Bring the contents of the wok to the boil, then simmer gently for 3–4 minutes, or until the chicken and vegetables are tender. Remove from the heat and tip into a warmed serving dish. Garnish with chopped coriander and serve immediately with boiled or steamed rice.

Thai Chicken Fried Rice

SERVES 2

125 g/4 oz skinless, boneless chicken breast
2 tbsp vegetable oil
2 garlic cloves, peeled and finely chopped
1–2 tsp, depending on taste,

medium curry paste
225 g/8 oz cold cooked rice
1 tbsp light soy sauce
1 tbsp Thai fish sauce
large pinch sugar
freshly ground black pepper

To garnish:
2 spring onions, trimmed and shredded lengthways
½ small onion, peeled and very finely sliced

Using a sharp knife, trim the chicken, discarding any sinew or fat, and cut into small cubes. Reserve.

Heat a wok or large frying pan, add the oil and, when hot, add the garlic and cook for 10–20 seconds, or until just golden. Add the curry paste and stir-fry for a few seconds. Add the chicken and stir-fry for 3–4 minutes, or until tender and the chicken has turned white.

Stir the cold cooked rice into the chicken mixture, then add the soy sauce, fish sauce and sugar, stirring well after each addition. Stir-fry for 2–3 minutes, or until the chicken is cooked through and the rice is piping hot.

Check the seasoning and, if necessary, add a little extra soy sauce. Turn the rice and chicken mixture into a warmed serving dish. Season lightly with black pepper and garnish with shredded spring onion and onion slices. Serve immediately.

Thai Coconut Chicken

SERVES 2

½ tsp cumin seeds
½ tsp mustard seeds
½ tsp coriander seeds
½ tsp turmeric
1 bird's-eye chilli, deseeded and finely chopped
1 tbsp freshly grated root ginger

1 garlic clove, peeled and finely chopped
50 ml/2 fl oz double cream
4 skinless chicken thighs
2 tbsp groundnut oil
1 medium onion, peeled and finely sliced
150 ml/¼ pint coconut milk

salt and freshly ground black pepper
2–4 tbsp freshly chopped coriander
2 spring onions, shredded, to garnish
freshly cooked Thai fragrant rice, to serve

Heat the wok and add the cumin seeds, mustard seeds and coriander seeds. Dry-fry over a low to medium heat for 2 minutes, or until the fragrance becomes stronger and the seeds start to pop. Add the turmeric and leave to cool slightly. Grind the spices in a pestle and mortar, or blend to a fine powder in a food processor.

Mix the chilli, ginger, garlic and the cream together in a small bowl, add the ground spices and mix. Place the chicken thighs in a shallow dish and spread the spice paste over the thighs.

Heat the wok over a high heat, add the oil and, when hot, add the onion and stir-fry until golden brown. Add the chicken and the spice paste. Cook for 5–6 minutes, stirring occasionally, until evenly coloured. Add the coconut milk and season to taste with salt and pepper. Simmer the chicken for 15–20 minutes, or until the thighs are cooked through, taking care not to allow the mixture to boil. Stir in the chopped coriander and serve immediately with the freshly cooked rice sprinkled with shredded spring onions.

Chicken & Baby Vegetable Stir–fry

SERVES 2

1 tbsp groundnut oil
1 small red chilli, deseeded and finely chopped
150 g/5 oz chicken breast or thigh meat, skinned and cut into cubes
2 baby leeks, trimmed and sliced
6 asparagus spears, halved

50 g/2 oz mangetout, trimmed
75 g/3 oz baby carrots, trimmed and halved lengthways
75 g/3 oz fine green beans, trimmed and diagonally sliced
50 g/2 oz baby sweetcorn,

diagonally halved
50 ml/2 fl oz chicken stock
2 tsp light soy sauce
1 tsp dry sherry
1 tsp sesame oil
toasted sesame seeds, to garnish

Heat the wok until very hot and add the oil. Add the chopped chilli and chicken and stir-fry for 2–3 minutes, or until the chicken is golden.

Add the leeks to the chicken and stir-fry for 2 minutes. Add the asparagus spears, mangetout, baby carrots, green beans and baby sweetcorn. Stir-fry for 3–4 minutes, or until the vegetables soften slightly but still retain a slight crispness.

In a small bowl, mix together the chicken stock, soy sauce, dry sherry and sesame oil. Pour into the wok, stir and cook until heated through. Sprinkle with the toasted sesame seeds and serve immediately.

Chicken with Noodles

SERVES 2

225 g/8 oz medium
   egg noodles
125 g/4 oz skinless, boneless
   chicken breast fillets
1 tbsp light soy sauce
2 tsp Chinese rice wine or

dry sherry
5 tsp groundnut oil
2 garlic cloves, peeled and
   finely chopped
50 g/2 oz mangetout
25 g/1 oz smoked back

bacon, cut into fine strips
½ tsp sugar
2 spring onions, peeled and
   finely chopped
1 tsp sesame oil

Cook the noodles according to the packet instructions. Drain and refresh under cold water. Drain again and reserve.

Slice the chicken into fine shreds and mix with 2 teaspoons of the light soy sauce and the Chinese rice wine. Leave to marinate in the refrigerator for 10 minutes.

Heat a wok, add 2 teaspoons of the oil and, when hot, stir-fry the chicken shreds for about 2 minutes, then transfer to a plate. Wipe the wok clean with absorbent kitchen paper.

Return the wok to the heat and add the remaining oil. Add the garlic, then after 10 seconds add the mangetout and bacon. Stir-fry for a further 1 minute, then add the drained noodles, remaining soy sauce, sugar and spring onions. Stir-fry for a further 2 minutes, then add the reserved chicken.

Stir-fry for a further 3–4 minutes until the chicken is cooked through. Add the sesame oil and mix together. Serve either hot or cold.

Chicken Wraps

For the stir-fried chicken:
2 skinless chicken breast
   fillets
finely grated zest and juice
   of 1 lime
2 tsp caster sugar
1 tsp dried oregano
½ tsp ground cinnamon
¼ tsp cayenne pepper

2 tbsp sunflower oil
1 onion, peeled and sliced
1 small green, 1 red and 1
   yellow pepper, deseeded
   and sliced
salt and freshly ground
   black pepper

For the tortillas:
125 g/4½ oz plain flour
pinch salt
scant ¼ tsp baking powder
25 g/1 oz white vegetable fat

To serve:
sour cream
guacamole

Slice the chicken across the grain into 2 cm/¾ inch wide strips. Place in a bowl with the lime zest and juice, sugar, oregano, cinnamon and cayenne pepper. Mix well and leave to marinate while making the tortillas.

Sift the flour, salt and baking powder into a bowl. Rub in the white fat, then sprinkle over 4 tablespoons of warm water and mix to a stiff dough. Knead on a lightly floured surface for 10 minutes until smooth and elastic. Divide the dough into 6 equal pieces and roll out each to a 15 cm/6 inch circle. Cover with clingfilm to prevent them drying out before you cook them. Heat a nonstick wok and cook each tortilla for about 1 minute on each side, or until golden and slightly blistered. Remove the tortillas and keep them warm and pliable in a clean tea towel.

Heat 1 tablespoon of the oil in the wok and stir-fry the onion for 5 minutes until lightly coloured. Remove with a slotted spoon and reserve.

Add the remaining oil to the wok and heat. Drain the chicken from the marinade and add it to the wok. Stir-fry for 5 minutes, then return the onions, add the pepper slices and cook for a further 3–4 minutes, or until the chicken is cooked through and the vegetables are tender. Season to taste with salt and pepper and serve with the tortillas, sour cream and guacamole.

Chicken & Asparagus with Tagliatelle

SERVES 2

125 g/4 oz fresh asparagus
25 g/1 oz butter
3 spring onions, trimmed
   and coarsely chopped
175 g/6 oz boneless, skinless

chicken breast, thinly sliced
1 tbsp white vermouth
175 ml/6 fl oz double cream
1 tbsp freshly snipped chives
225 g/8 oz fresh tagliatelle

25 g/1 oz Parmesan or
   pecorino cheese, grated
snipped chives, to garnish
extra Parmesan cheese
   (optional), to serve

Using a swivel-bladed vegetable peeler, lightly peel the asparagus spears and then cook in lightly salted, boiling water for 2–3 minutes, or until just tender. Drain and refresh in cold water, then cut into 4 cm/1½ inch pieces and reserve.

Melt the butter in a large frying pan, then add the spring onions and the chicken and fry for 4 minutes. Add the vermouth and allow to reduce until the liquid has evaporated. Pour in the cream and half the chives. Cook gently for 5–7 minutes until the sauce has thickened and slightly reduced and the chicken is tender.

Bring a large saucepan of lightly salted water to the boil and cook the tagliatelle for 4–5 minutes, or until *al dente*. Drain and immediately add to the chicken and cream sauce.

Using a pair of spaghetti tongs or kitchen forks, lightly toss the sauce and pasta until it is mixed thoroughly. Add the remaining chives and the Parmesan cheese and toss gently. Garnish with snipped chives and serve immediately, with extra Parmesan cheese, if you like.

Mini Chicken Balls with Tagliatelle

SERVES 2

225 g/8 oz fresh chicken
   mince
25 g/1 oz sun-dried tomatoes,
   drained and finely
chopped salt and freshly
   ground black pepper

1 g/½ oz butter
175 g/6 oz leeks, trimmed
   and diagonally sliced
50 g/2 oz frozen broad beans
200 ml/7 fl oz single cream
25 g/1 oz freshly grated

Parmesan cheese
175 g/6 oz tagliatelle
2 medium eggs
fresh herbs, to garnish

Mix the chicken and tomatoes together and season to taste with salt and pepper. Divide the mixture into 16 pieces and roll into balls. Transfer to a baking sheet, cover and leave in the refrigerator for 1 hour.

Melt the butter in a large frying pan, add the chicken balls and cook for 5 minutes, or until golden, turning occasionally. Remove, drain on absorbent kitchen paper and keep warm.

Add the leeks and broad beans to the frying pan and cook, stirring, for 10 minutes, or until cooked and tender. Return the chicken balls to the pan, then stir in the cream and Parmesan cheese and heat through.

Meanwhile, bring a large pan of lightly salted water to a rolling boil. Add the pasta and cook according to the packet instructions, or until *al dente*.

Bring a separate frying pan full of water to the boil, crack in the eggs and simmer for 2–4 minutes, or until poached to personal preference.

Meanwhile, drain the pasta thoroughly and return to the pan. Pour the chicken ball and vegetable sauce over the pasta, toss lightly and heat through for 1–2 minutes. Arrange on warmed individual plates and top with the poached eggs. Garnish with fresh herbs and serve.

Spicy Chicken & Pasta Salad

175 g/6 oz pasta shells
15 g/½ oz butter
1 small onion, peeled
    and chopped
1 tbsp mild curry paste
50 g/2 oz ready-to-eat dried
    apricots, chopped

1 tbsp tomato paste
2 tbsp mango chutney
200 ml/7 fl oz mayonnaise
200 g/7 oz can pineapple
    slices in fruit juice
salt and freshly ground
    black pepper

175 g/6 oz skinned and
    boned cooked chicken,
    cut into bite-sized pieces
1 tbsp flaked toasted
    almond slivers
coriander sprigs, to garnish

Bring a large pan of lightly salted water to a rolling boil. Add the pasta shells and cook according to the packet instructions, or until *al dente*. Drain and refresh under cold running water, then drain thoroughly and place in a large serving bowl.

Meanwhile, melt the butter in a heavy-based pan, add the onion and cook for 5 minutes, or until softened. Add the curry paste and cook, stirring, for 2 minutes. Stir in the apricots and tomato paste, then cook for 1 minute. Remove from the heat and allow to cool.

Blend the mango chutney and mayonnaise together in a small bowl. Drain the pineapple slices, adding 2 tablespoons of the pineapple juice to the mayonnaise mixture; reserve the pineapple slices. Season the mayonnaise to taste with salt and pepper.

Cut the pineapple slices into chunks and stir into the pasta together with the mayonnaise mixture, curry mixture and cooked chicken pieces. Toss lightly together to coat the pasta. Sprinkle with the almond slivers, garnish with coriander sprigs and serve.

Turkey Hash with Potato & Beetroot

SERVES 2

1 tbsp vegetable oil
50 g/2 oz butter
2 slices streaky bacon, rind removed, and chopped
1 small onion, peeled and finely chopped

225 g/8 oz cooked turkey, diced
225 g/8 oz finely chopped cooked potatoes
1–2 tbsp freshly chopped parsley

1 tbsp plain flour
125 g/4 oz cooked beetroot, diced
green salad, to serve

In a large heavy-based frying pan, heat the oil and half the butter over a medium heat until sizzling. Add the bacon and cook for 4 minutes, or until crisp and golden, stirring occasionally. Using a slotted spoon, transfer to a large bowl. Add the onion to the pan and cook for 3–4 minutes, or until soft and golden, stirring frequently.

Meanwhile, add the turkey, potatoes, parsley and flour to the cooked bacon in the bowl. Stir and toss gently, then fold in the diced beetroot.

Add half the remaining butter to the frying pan and then the turkey vegetable mixture. Stir, then spread the mixture to evenly cover the bottom of the frying pan. Cook for 15 minutes, or until the underside is crisp and brown, pressing the hash firmly into a cake with a spatula. Remove from the heat.

Invert a large plate over the frying pan and, holding the plate and frying pan together with an oven glove, turn the hash out onto the plate. Heat the remaining butter in the pan, slide the hash back into the pan and cook for 4 minutes, or until crisp and brown on the other side. Invert onto the plate again and serve immediately with a green salad.

HELPFUL HINT
Make sure that you buy plainly cooked beetroot, rather than the type preserved in vinegar.

Turkey with Oriental Mushrooms

15 g/½ oz dried Chinese
  mushrooms
225 g/8 oz turkey breast
  steaks
85 ml/3 fl oz turkey or
  chicken stock
2 tbsp groundnut oil
1 small red pepper,

deseeded and sliced
125 g/4 oz sugar snap peas,
  trimmed
50 g/2 oz shiitake
  mushrooms, wiped
  and halved
50 g/2 oz oyster mushrooms,
  wiped and halved

1 tbsp yellow bean sauce
1–2 tbsp soy sauce
1 tbsp, or to taste, hot
  chilli sauce
freshly cooked noodles,
  to serve

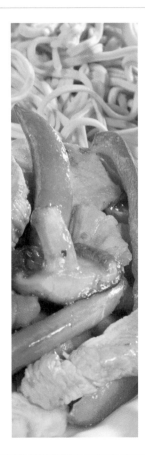

Place the dried mushrooms in a small bowl, cover with almost boiling water and leave for 20–30 minutes. Drain and discard any woody stems from the mushrooms. Cut the turkey and into thin strips.

Pour the turkey or chicken stock into a wok or large frying pan and bring to the boil. Add the turkey and cook gently for 3 minutes, or until the turkey is sealed completely, then, using a slotted spoon, remove from the wok and reserve. Discard any stock.

Wipe the wok clean and reheat, then add the oil. When the oil is almost smoking, add the drained turkey and stir-fry for 2 minutes.

Add the drained mushrooms to the wok with the red pepper, the sugar snap peas and the shiitake and oyster mushrooms. Stir-fry for 2 minutes, then add the yellow bean, soy and hot chilli sauces.

Stir-fry the mixture for 1–2 more minutes, or until the turkey is cooked thoroughly and the vegetables are cooked but still retain a bite. Turn into a warmed serving dish and serve immediately with freshly cooked noodles.

Turkey Escalopes Marsala with Wilted Watercress

SERVES 2

2 turkey escalopes, each about 150 g/5 oz
15 g/½ oz plain flour
½ tsp dried thyme
salt and freshly ground

black pepper
1–2 tbsp olive oil
50 g/2 oz watercress
25 g/1 oz butter
12 g/4 oz mushrooms,

wiped and quartered
50 ml/2 fl oz dry Marsala wine
50 ml/2 fl oz chicken stock or water

Place each turkey escalope between 2 sheets of nonstick baking parchment and, using a meat mallet or rolling pin, pound to make an escalope about 3 mm/⅛ inch thick. Put the flour in a shallow dish, add the thyme, season to taste with salt and pepper and stir to blend. Coat each escalope lightly on both sides with the flour mixture, then reserve.

Heat the olive oil in a large frying pan, add the watercress and stir-fry for about 1–2 minutes, until just wilted and brightly coloured. Season with salt and pepper. Using a slotted spoon, transfer the watercress to a plate and keep warm.

Add half the butter to the frying pan and, when melted, add the mushrooms. Stir-fry for 4 minutes, or until golden and tender. Remove from the pan and reserve.

Add the remaining butter to the pan and cook the flour-coated escalopes for 2–3 minutes on each side, or until golden and cooked thoroughly, adding the remaining oil, if necessary. Remove from the pan and keep warm.

Add the Marsala wine to the pan and stir, scraping up any browned bits from the bottom. Add the stock or water and bring to the boil over a high heat. Season lightly. Return the escalopes and mushrooms to the pan and reheat gently until piping hot. Divide the warm watercress between two serving plates. Arrange 1 escalope over each serving of wilted watercress and spoon over the mushrooms and Marsala sauce. Serve immediately.

Vegetables

Creamy Vegetable Korma

SERVES 2

2 tbsp ghee or unsalted butter
1 small onion, peeled and chopped
2 garlic cloves, peeled and crushed
1 cm/½ inch piece root ginger, peeled and grated
2 cardamom pods
1 tsp ground coriander
½ tsp ground cumin
½ tsp ground turmeric
finely grated zest and juice of ½ lemon
25 g/1 oz ground almonds
300 ml/½ pint vegetable stock
225 g/8 oz potatoes, peeled and diced
225 g/8 oz mixed vegetables, such as cauliflower, carrots and turnip, cut into chunks
75 ml/3 fl oz double cream
1 tbsp freshly chopped coriander
salt and freshly ground black pepper
naan bread, to serve

Heat the ghee or butter in a large saucepan. Add the onion and cook for 5 minutes. Stir in the garlic and ginger and cook for a further 5 minutes, or until soft and just beginning to colour.

Stir in the cardamom, ground coriander, cumin and turmeric. Continue cooking over a low heat for 1 minute, stirring.

Stir in the lemon zest and juice and almonds. Blend in the vegetable stock. Slowly bring to the boil, stirring occasionally.

Add the potatoes and vegetables. Bring back to the boil, then reduce the heat, cover and simmer for 35–40 minutes, or until the vegetables are just tender. Check after 25 minutes and add a little more stock if needed.

Slowly stir in the cream and chopped coriander. Season to taste with salt and pepper. Cook very gently until heated through, but do not boil. Serve immediately with naan bread.

HELPFUL HINT

When buying for two, buy in small amounts; this way the vegetables will not lose their nutrients by the time you come to eat them.

Thai–style Cauliflower & Potato Curry

SERVES 2

225 g/8 oz new potatoes, peeled and halved or quartered
175 g/6 oz cauliflower florets
1–2 garlic cloves, peeled and crushed
1 small onion, peeled and finely chopped

25 g/1 oz ground almonds
½ tsp ground coriander
pinch, or to taste, ground cumin
½ tsp turmeric
2 tbsp groundnut oil
salt and freshly ground black pepper

25 g/1 oz creamed coconut, broken into small pieces
200 ml/7 fl oz vegetable stock
1 tbsp mango chutney
fresh coriander sprigs, to garnish
freshly cooked long-grain rice, to serve

Bring a saucepan of lightly salted water to the boil, add the potatoes and cook for 15 minutes, or until just tender. Drain and leave to cool. Boil the cauliflower for 2 minutes, then drain and refresh under cold running water. Drain again and reserve.

Meanwhile, blend the garlic, onion, ground almonds and spices with 1 tablespoon of the oil and salt and pepper to taste in a food processor until a smooth paste is formed. Heat a wok, add the remaining oil and, when hot, add the spice paste and cook for 3–4 minutes, stirring continuously.

Dissolve the creamed coconut in 3 tablespoons of boiling water and add to the wok. Pour in the stock, cook for 2–3 minutes, then stir in the cooked potatoes and cauliflower.

Stir in the mango chutney and heat through for 3–4 minutes, or until piping hot. Tip into a warmed serving dish, garnish with freshly chopped coriander and serve with freshly cooked rice.

HELPFUL HINT

Often it is difficult to buy small amounts of potatoes. If this is the case, store in either brown paper bags or potato bags which are available from kitchenware shops.

Calypso Rice with Curried Bananas

SERVES 2

2 tbsp sunflower oil
1 small onion, peeled
   and finely chopped
1 garlic clove, peeled
   and crushed
1 red chilli, deseeded and
   finely chopped
1small red pepper,
   deseeded and chopped

175 g/6 oz basmati rice
juice of 1 lime
scant 600 ml/1 pint
   vegetable stock
75 g/3 oz canned black-eye
   beans, drained and rinsed
1 tbsp freshly chopped
   parsley
salt and freshly ground

black pepper
coriander sprigs, to garnish

For the curried bananas:
2 green bananas
1 tbsp sunflower oil
1–2 tsp mild curry paste
85 ml/3 fl oz coconut milk

Heat the oil in a large frying pan and gently cook the onion for 10 minutes until soft. Add the garlic, chilli and red pepper and cook for 2–3 minutes.

Rinse the rice under cold running water, then add to the pan and stir. Pour in the lime juice and stock, bring to the boil, cover and simmer for 12–15 minutes, or until the rice is tender and the stock is absorbed. Stir in the black-eye beans and chopped parsley and season to taste with salt and pepper. Leave to stand, covered, for 5 minutes before serving, to allow the beans to warm through.

While the rice is cooking, make the curried green bananas. Remove the skins from the bananas – they may need to be cut off with a sharp knife. Slice the flesh thickly. Heat the oil in a frying pan and cook the bananas, in 2 batches, for 2–3 minutes, or until lightly browned.

Pour the coconut milk into a pan and stir in the curry paste. Add the banana slices to the coconut milk and simmer, uncovered, over a low heat for 8–10 minutes, or until the bananas are very soft and the coconut milk slightly reduced. Spoon the rice onto warmed serving plates, garnish with coriander and serve immediately with the curried bananas.

Spring Vegetable & Herb Risotto

600 ml/1 pint vegetable stock
125 g/4 oz asparagus tips, trimmed
125 g/4 oz baby carrots, scrubbed
50 g/2 oz peas, fresh or frozen
50 g/2 oz fine French beans, trimmed

1 tbsp olive oil
1 onion, peeled and finely chopped
1 garlic clove, peeled and finely chopped
2 tsp freshly chopped thyme
175 g/6 oz risotto rice
50 ml/2 fl oz white wine

1 tsp each freshly chopped basil, chives and parsley
grated zest of ½ lemon
1–2 tbsp crème fraîche
salt and freshly ground black pepper

Bring the vegetable stock to the boil in a large saucepan and add the asparagus, baby carrots, peas and beans. Bring the stock back to the boil and remove the vegetables at once using a slotted spoon. Rinse under cold running water. Drain again and reserve. Keep the stock hot.

Heat the oil in a large deep frying pan and add the onion. Cook over a medium heat for 4–5 minutes until starting to brown. Add the garlic and thyme and cook for a further few seconds. Add the rice and stir well for a minute until the rice is hot and coated in oil.

Add the white wine and stir constantly until the wine is almost completely absorbed by the rice. Begin adding the stock a ladleful at a time, stirring well and waiting until the last ladleful has been absorbed before stirring in the next. Add the vegetables after using about half of the stock. Continue until all the stock is used. This will take 20–25 minutes. The rice and vegetables should be tender.

Remove the pan from the heat. Stir in the herbs, lemon zest and crème fraîche. Season to taste with salt and pepper and serve immediately.

Rice–filled Peppers

SERVES 2

4 ripe tomatoes
1 tbsp olive oil
1 small onion, peeled
   and chopped
1 garlic clove, peeled
   and crushed
½ tsp dark muscovado sugar

50 g/2 oz cooked long-
   grain rice
25 g/1 oz pine nuts, toasted
1 tbsp freshly chopped
   oregano
salt and freshly ground
   black pepper

2 large peppers

To serve:
mixed salad
crusty bread

Preheat the oven to 200°C/400°F/Gas Mark 6. Put the tomatoes in a small bowl and pour over boiling water to cover. Leave for 1 minute, then drain. Plunge the tomatoes into cold water to cool, then peel off the skins. Quarter, remove the seeds and chop.

Heat the olive oil in a frying pan and cook the onion gently for 10 minutes until softened. Add the garlic, chopped tomatoes and sugar.

Gently cook the tomato mixture for 10 minutes until thickened. Remove from the heat and stir the rice, pine nuts and oregano into the sauce. Season to taste with salt and pepper.

Halve the peppers lengthways, cutting through and leaving the stem on. Remove the seeds and cores, then put the peppers in a lightly oiled roasting tin, cut-side down, and cook in the preheated oven for about 10 minutes.

Turn the peppers so they are cut-side up. Spoon in the filling, then cover with kitchen foil. Return to the oven for 15 minutes, or until the peppers are very tender, removing the foil for the last 5 minutes to allow the tops to brown a little.

Serve with a mixed salad and plenty of warm, crusty bread.

Chef's Rice Salad

SERVES 2

125 g/4 oz wild rice
¼ cucumber
75 g/3 oz cherry tomatoes
3 spring onions, trimmed
3 tbsp extra-virgin olive oil
1 tbsp balsamic vinegar
½–1 tsp Dijon mustard

1 tsp caster sugar
salt and freshly ground
  black pepper
50 g/2 oz rocket
75 g/3 oz back bacon
50 g/2 oz cooked chicken
  meat, finely diced

50 g/2 oz Emmenthal
  cheese, grated
50 g/2 oz large cooked
  prawns, peeled
1 avocado, stoned, peeled
  and sliced, to garnish
warm crusty bread, to serve

Put the rice in a saucepan of water and bring to the boil, stirring once or twice. Reduce the heat, cover and simmer gently for 30–50 minutes, depending on the texture you prefer. Drain well and reserve.

Thinly peel the cucumber, cut in half, then, using a teaspoon, remove the seeds. Cut the cucumber into thin slices. Cut the tomatoes in quarters. Cut the spring onions into diagonal slices.

Whisk the olive oil with the vinegar, then whisk in the mustard and sugar. Season to taste with salt and pepper.

In a large bowl, gently toss together the cooled rice with the tomatoes, cucumber, spring onions and the rocket. Pour over the dressing and toss lightly together.

Heat a griddle pan and, when hot, cook the bacon on both sides for 4–6 minutes, or until crisp. Remove and chop. Arrange the prepared rocket salad on a platter, then arrange the bacon, chicken, cheese and prawns on top. Toss if wished. Garnish with avocado slices and serve with plenty of warm, crusty bread.

Huevos Rancheros

1 tbsp olive oil
1 small onion, peeled and
    finely chopped
1 small red pepper,
    deseeded and finely
    chopped
2 garlic cloves, peeled and
    finely chopped
1–2 green chillies, deseeded
    and finely chopped

½ tsp ground cumin
½–1 tsp, depending on taste,
    chilli powder
1 tsp ground coriander
350 g/12 oz ripe plum
    tomatoes, peeled,
    deseeded and roughly
    chopped
¼ tsp sugar
4 small eggs

2–4 flour tortillas
1 tbsp freshly chopped
    coriander
salt and freshly ground
    black pepper
fresh coriander sprigs,
    to garnish
refried beans, to serve
    (optional)

Heat the oil in a large heavy-based saucepan. Add the onion and pepper and cook over a medium heat for 10 minutes. Add the garlic, chillies, ground cumin, chilli powder and ground coriander and cook for a further minute. Add the tomatoes and sugar. Stir well, cover and cook gently for 20 minutes. Uncover and cook for a further 20 minutes.

Lightly poach the eggs in a large frying pan filled with gently simmering water. Drain well and keep warm.

Place the tortillas briefly under a preheated hot grill. Turn once, then remove from the grill when crisp.

Add the freshly chopped coriander to the tomato sauce and season to taste with salt and pepper.

To serve, arrange two tortillas on each serving plate, top with two eggs and spoon the sauce over. Garnish with sprigs of fresh coriander and serve immediately with warmed refried beans, if liked.

Stuffed Onions with Pine Nuts

SERVES 2

2 medium onions, peeled
1–2 garlic cloves, peeled
   and crushed
1 tbsp fresh brown
   breadcrumbs
1 tbsp white breadcrumbs

15 g/½ oz sultanas
15 g/½ oz pine nuts
25 g/1 oz hard cheese, such
   as Edam, grated
1 tbsp freshly chopped
   parsley

1 medium egg yolk, beaten
salt and freshly ground
   black pepper
salad leaves, to serve

Preheat the oven to 200°C/400°F/Gas Mark 6. Bring a pan of water to the boil, add the onions and cook gently for about 15 minutes.

Drain well. Allow the onions to cool, then slice each one in half horizontally.

Scoop out most of the onion flesh but leave a reasonably firm shell.

Chop up 2 tablespoons of the onion flesh and place in a bowl with the crushed garlic, breadcrumbs, sultanas, pine nuts, grated cheese and parsley.

Mix the breadcrumb mixture together thoroughly. Bind together with as much of the beaten egg as necessary to make a firm filling. Season to taste with salt and pepper.

Pile the mixture back into the onion shells and top with the grated cheese. Place on an oiled baking tray and cook in the preheated oven for 20–30 minutes, or until golden brown. Serve immediately with the salad leaves.

Carrot, Celeriac & Sesame Seed Salad

SERVES 2

125 g/4 oz celeriac
125 g/4 oz carrots, peeled
25 g/1 oz seedless raisins
1 tbsp sesame seeds
freshly chopped parsley,
    to garnish

**For the lemon-and-chilli
    dressing:**
2 tsp finely grated lemon zest
2 tbsp lemon juice
2 tbsp sunflower oil
2 tsp clear honey

1 red bird's-eye chilli,
    deseeded and finely
    chopped
salt and freshly ground
    black pepper

Slice the celeriac into thin matchsticks. Place in a small saucepan of boiling salted water and boil for 2 minutes.

Drain and rinse the celeriac in cold water and place in a mixing bowl.

Finely grate the carrot(s). Add the carrot and the raisins to the celeriac in the bowl.

Place the sesame seeds under a hot grill or dry-fry in a frying pan for 1 minute until golden brown, then leave to cool.

Make the dressing by whisking together the lemon zest, lemon juice, oil, honey, chilli and seasoning or by shaking thoroughly in a screw-top jar.

Pour half the dressing over the salad and toss well. Turn into a serving dish and sprinkle over the toasted sesame seeds and chopped parsley. Serve the remaining dressing separately.

Stir-fried Greens

SERVES 2

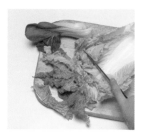

225 g/8 oz Chinese leaves
125 g/4 oz pak choi
125 g/4 oz broccoli florets
1 tbsp sesame seeds
1 tbsp groundnut oil
1 tbsp fresh root ginger,
    peeled and finely chopped

1–2 garlic cloves, peeled
    and finely chopped
1 red chilli, deseeded and
    split in half
25 ml/1 fl oz chicken stock
1 tbsp Chinese rice wine
1 tsp dark soy sauce

1 tsp light soy sauce
1 tsp black bean sauce
freshly ground black pepper
1 tsp sugar
1 tsp sesame oil

Separate the Chinese leaves and pak choi and wash well. Cut into 2.5 cm/1 inch strips. Separate the broccoli into small florets. Heat a wok or large frying pan, add the sesame seeds and stir-fry for 30 seconds, or until browned.

Add the oil to the wok and, when hot, add the ginger, garlic and chilli and stir-fry for 30 seconds. Add the broccoli and stir-fry for 1 minute. Add the Chinese leaves and pak choi and stir-fry for a further 1 minute.

Pour the chicken stock and Chinese rice wine into the wok with the soy and black bean sauces. Season to taste with pepper and add the sugar. Reduce the heat and simmer for 6–8 minutes, or until the vegetables are tender but still firm to the bite. Tip into a warmed serving dish, removing the chilli if preferred. Drizzle with the sesame oil and serve immediately.

Bean & Cashew Stir–fry

SERVES 2

2 tbsp sunflower oil
1 small onion, peeled and
  finely chopped
1 celery stalk, trimmed
  and chopped
1 cm/½ inch piece fresh root
  ginger, peeled and grated
2 garlic cloves, peeled
  and crushed

1 red chilli, deseeded and
  finely chopped
75 g/3 oz fine French beans,
  trimmed and halved
75 g/3 oz mangetout,
  sliced diagonally into 3
50 g/2 oz unsalted
  cashew nuts
1 tsp brown sugar

50 ml/2 fl oz vegetable stock
1 tbsp dry sherry
2 tsp light soy sauce
1 tsp red wine vinegar
salt and freshly ground
  black pepper
freshly chopped coriander,
  to garnish

Heat a wok or large frying pan, add the oil and, when hot, add the onion and celery and stir-fry gently for 3–4 minutes, or until softened.

Add the ginger, garlic and chilli to the wok and stir-fry for 30 seconds. Stir in the French beans and mangetout together with the cashew nuts and continue to stir-fry for 1–2 minutes, or until the nuts are golden brown.

Dissolve the sugar in the stock, then blend with the sherry, soy sauce and vinegar. Stir into the bean mixture and bring to the boil. Simmer gently, stirring occasionally, for 3–4 minutes, or until the beans and mangetout are tender but still crisp and the sauce has thickened slightly. Season to taste with salt and pepper. Transfer to a warmed serving bowl or spoon onto individual plates. Sprinkle with freshly chopped coriander and serve immediately.

Spring Rolls with Mixed Vegetables

1 tbsp sesame oil
50 g/2 oz broccoli florets, cut into small pieces
50 g/2 oz carrots, peeled and cut into matchsticks
50 g/2 oz courgettes, cut into strips
50 g/2 oz button mushrooms, finely chopped
1 cm/½ inch piece fresh root ginger, peeled and grated
1 garlic clove, peeled and finely chopped
2 spring onions, trimmed and finely chopped
25 g/1 oz beansprouts
1 tsp light soy sauce
pinch cayenne pepper
2 tbsp plain flour
6 sheets filo pastry
300 ml/½ pint groundnut oil
spring onion curls, to garnish

Heat a wok, add the sesame oil and, when hot, add the broccoli, carrots, courgettes, mushrooms, ginger, garlic and spring onions and stir-fry for 1–2 minutes, or until slightly softened.

Turn into a bowl, add the beansprouts, soy sauce and cayenne pepper and mix together. Transfer the vegetables to a colander and drain for 5 minutes. Meanwhile, blend the flour with 1–2 tablespoons of water to form a paste and reserve.

Fold a sheet of filo pastry in half and in half again, brushing a little water between each layer. Place a spoonful of the drained vegetable mixture on the pastry. Brush a little of the flour paste along the edges. Turn the edges into the centre, then roll up and seal. Repeat with the rest.

Wipe the wok clean, return to the heat, add the oil and heat to 190°C/375°F. Add the spring rolls in batches and deep-fry for 2–3 minutes, or until golden. Drain on absorbent kitchen paper, arrange on a platter, garnish with spring onion curls and serve immediately.

TASTY TIP

For lower-fat spring rolls, lightly brush with groundnut oil and cook on a baking sheet in the centre of a preheated oven at 190°C/375°F/Gas Mark 5 for 10 minutes, or until golden and crisp.

Crispy Pancake Rolls

SERVES 2

150 g/5 oz plain flour
pinch salt
1 small egg
2 tsp sunflower oil
1 tbsp light olive oil
1 cm/½ inch piece fresh root
    ginger, peeled and grated
1 garlic clove, peeled

and crushed
125 g/4 oz tofu, drained and
    cut into small dice
1 tbsp soy sauce
1 tsp dry sherry
75 g/3 oz button
    mushrooms, wiped
    and chopped

1 small celery stalk, trimmed
    and finely chopped
1 spring onion, trimmed and
    finely chopped
300 ml/½ pint groundnut oil
fresh coriander sprig
    and sliced spring onion,
    to garnish

HELPFUL HINT

The pancakes can be made up to 24 hours before needed. Place them in a single layer on a plate, cover with clingfilm and refrigerate. Leave at room temperature for about 30 minutes before frying.

Sift 125 g/4 oz of the flour with the salt into a large bowl, make a well in the centre and drop in the egg. Beat to form a smooth, thin batter, gradually adding 150 ml/¼ pint water and drawing in the flour from the sides of the bowl. Mix the remaining flour with 1–2 tablespoons of water to make a thick paste. Reserve.

Heat a little sunflower oil in a 20.5 cm/8 inch omelette or frying pan and pour in 2 tablespoons of the batter. Cook for 1–2 minutes, flip over and cook for a further 1–2 minutes, or until firm. Slide from the pan and keep warm. Make more pancakes with the remaining batter.

Heat a wok or large frying pan, add the olive oil and, when hot, add the ginger, garlic and tofu, stir-fry for 30 seconds, then pour in the soy sauce and sherry. Add the mushrooms, celery and spring onion. Stir-fry for 1–2 minutes, then remove from the wok and leave to cool.

Place a little filling in the centre of each pancake. Brush the edges with the flour paste, fold in the edges, then roll up into parcels. Heat the groundnut oil to 180°C/350°F in the wok. Fry the pancake rolls for 2–3 minutes, or until golden. Serve immediately, garnished with chopped spring onions and a sprig of coriander.

Chargrilled Vegetable & Goats' Cheese Pizza

SERVES 2 TO SHARE

125 g/4 oz baking potato
1 tbsp olive oil
225 g/8 oz strong white flour
½ tsp salt
1 tsp easy-blend dried yeast

For the topping:
1 medium aubergine,
   thinly sliced

2 small courgettes, trimmed
   and sliced lengthways
1 yellow pepper, quartered
   and deseeded
1 red onion, peeled and sliced
   into very thin wedges
5 tbsp olive oil
175 g/6 oz cooked new
   potatoes, halved

400 g/14 oz can chopped
   tomatoes, drained
2 tsp freshly chopped
   oregano
125 g/4 oz mozzarella cheese,
   cut into small cubes
125 g/4 oz goats' cheese,
   crumbled

Preheat the oven to 220°C/425°F/Gas Mark 7, 15 minutes before baking. Put a baking sheet in the oven to heat up. Cook the potato in lightly salted boiling water until tender. Peel and mash with the olive oil until smooth.

Sift the flour and salt into a bowl. Stir in the yeast. Add the mashed potato and 150 ml/¼ pint warm water and mix to a soft dough. Knead for 5–6 minutes until smooth. Put the dough in a bowl, cover with clingfilm and leave to rise in a warm place for 30 minutes.

To make the topping, arrange the aubergine, courgettes, pepper and onion skin-side up on a grill rack and brush with 4 tablespoons of the oil. Grill for 4–5 minutes. Turn the vegetables and brush with the remaining oil. Grill for 3–4 minutes. Cool, skin and slice the pepper. Put all of the vegetables in a bowl, add the halved new potatoes and toss gently together. Set aside.

Briefly re-knead the dough, then roll out to a 30.5–35.5 cm/12–14 inch round, according to preferred thickness. Mix the tomatoes and oregano together and spread over the pizza base. Scatter over the mozzarella cheese. Put the pizza on the preheated baking sheet and bake for 8 minutes. Arrange the vegetables and goats' cheese on top and bake for 8–10 minutes. Serve.

Spinach, Pine Nut & Mascarpone Pizza

SERVES 2 TO SHARE

For basic pizza dough:
225 g/8 oz strong plain flour
½ tsp salt
¼ tsp quick-acting dried yeast
150 ml/¼ pint warm water
1 tbsp extra-virgin olive oil

For the topping:
3 tbsp olive oil
1 large red onion, peeled and chopped
2 garlic cloves, peeled and finely sliced
450 g/1 lb frozen spinach,
thawed and drained
salt and freshly ground black pepper
3 tbsp passata
125 g/4 oz mascarpone cheese
1 tbsp toasted pine nuts

Preheat the oven to 220°C/425°F/Gas Mark 7. Sift the flour and salt into a bowl and stir in the yeast. Make a well in the centre and gradually add the water and oil to form a soft dough.

Knead the dough on a floured surface for about 5 minutes until smooth and elastic. Place in a lightly oiled bowl and cover with clingfilm. Leave to rise in a warm place for 1 hour.

Knock the pizza dough with your fist a few times, shape and roll out thinly on a lightly floured board. Place on a lightly floured baking sheet and lift the edge to make a little rim. Place another baking sheet into the preheated oven to heat up.

Heat half the oil in a frying pan and gently fry the onion and garlic until soft and starting to change colour.

Squeeze out any excess water from the spinach and chop finely. Add to the onion and garlic with the remaining olive oil. Season to taste with salt and pepper.

Spread the passata on the pizza dough and top with the spinach mixture. Mix the mascarpone with the pine nuts and dot over the pizza. Slide the pizza onto the hot baking sheet and bake for 15–20 minutes. Transfer to a large plate and serve immediately.

Three Tomato Pizza

SERVES 2

1 quantity pizza dough (*see* page 194)
3 plum tomatoes
8 cherry tomatoes

6 sun-dried tomatoes
pinch sea salt
1 tbsp freshly chopped basil
2 tbsp extra-virgin olive oil

125 g/4 oz buffalo mozzarella cheese, sliced
freshly ground black pepper
fresh basil leaves, to garnish

Preheat the oven to 220°C/425°F/Gas Mark 7. Place two baking sheets into the oven to heat up.

Divide the prepared pizza dough in half.

Roll the pizza dough out on a lightly floured board to form 2 x 30 cm/12 inch rounds.

Slice the plum tomatoes, halve the cherry tomatoes and chop the sun-dried tomatoes into small pieces.

Divide all the tomatoes in half, then arrange on top of the two pizza bases and season to taste with the sea salt.

Sprinkle with the chopped basil and drizzle with the olive oil. Top with the mozzarella slices and season with black pepper.

Transfer the two pizzas onto the heated baking sheets and cook for 20–25 minutes, or until the cheese is golden brown and bubbling. If necessary, switch the trays so that they are both ready at the same time. Remove from the oven, garnish with the basil and serve.

Oriental Noodle & Peanut Salad with Coriander

SERVES 2

175 g/6 oz rice vermicelli
500 ml/18 fl oz light chicken
   stock or water
1 tsp sesame oil
1 tbsp light soy sauce
4 spring onions

2 tbsp groundnut oil
1 hot green chilli, deseeded
   and thinly sliced
1 tbsp roughly chopped
   coriander
1 tbsp freshly chopped mint

50 g/2 oz cucumber,
   finely chopped
25 g/1 oz beansprouts
40 g/1½ oz roasted peanuts,
   roughly chopped

Put the noodles into a large bowl. Bring the stock or water to the boil and immediately pour over the noodles. Leave to soak for 4 minutes, or according to the packet instructions. Drain well, discarding the liquid. Mix together the sesame oil and soy sauce and pour over the hot noodles. Toss well to coat and leave until cold.

Trim and thinly slice 2 of the spring onions. Heat the wok and then add the oil. Swirl the wok until lightly coated in the oil, then add the spring onions and, as soon as they sizzle, remove from the heat and leave to cool. When cold, toss with the noodles.

On a chopping board, cut the remaining spring onions lengthways 4–6 times, leave in a bowl of cold water until tassels form. Serve the noodles in individual bowls, each dressed with a little chilli, coriander, mint, cucumber, beansprouts and peanuts. Garnish with the spring onion tassels and serve.

Warm Noodle Salad with Sesame & Peanut Dressing

SERVES 2

50 g/2 oz smooth
    peanut butter
3 tbsp sesame oil
2 tbsp light soy sauce
1 tbsp red wine vinegar
2 tsp freshly grated
    root ginger

1 tbsp double cream
125 g/4 oz Chinese fine
    egg noodles
50 g/2 oz beansprouts
125 g/4 oz baby sweetcorn
50 g/2 oz carrots, peeled and
    cut into matchsticks

50 g/2 oz mangetout
50 g/2 oz cucumber, cut into
    thin strips
2 spring onions, trimmed
    and finely shredded

Place the peanut butter, 2 tablespoons of the sesame oil, the soy sauce, vinegar and ginger in a food processor. Blend until smooth, then stir in 2½ tablespoons hot water and blend again. Pour in the cream, blend briefly until smooth. Pour the dressing into a jug and reserve.

Bring a saucepan of lightly salted water to the boil, add the noodles and beansprouts and cook for 4 minutes, or according to the packet instructions. Drain, rinse under cold running water and drain again. Stir in the remaining sesame oil and keep warm.

Bring a saucepan of lightly salted water to the boil and add the baby sweetcorn, carrots and mangetout and cook for 3–4 minutes, or until just tender but still crisp. Drain and cut the mangetout in half. Slice the baby sweetcorn (if very large) into 2–3 pieces and arrange on a warmed serving dish with the noodles. Add the cucumber strips and spring onions. Spoon over a little of the dressing and serve immediately with the remaining dressing.

Pasta with Courgettes, Rosemary & Lemon

SERVES 2

175 g/6 oz dried pasta
  shapes, e.g. rigatoni
1 tbsp good-quality extra-
  virgin olive oil
2 garlic cloves, peeled and
  finely chopped
2 medium courgettes,
  thinly sliced

1 tbsp freshly chopped
  rosemary
1 tbsp freshly chopped
  parsley
grated zest and juice
  of 1 lemon
25 g/1 oz pitted black
  and green olives,

  roughly chopped
salt and freshly ground
  black pepper

To garnish:
lemon slices
fresh rosemary sprigs

Bring a large saucepan of salted water to the boil and add the pasta.

Return to the boil and cook until *al dente*, or according to the packet instructions.

Meanwhile, when the pasta is almost cooked, heat the oil in a large frying pan and add the garlic. Cook over a medium heat until the garlic just begins to brown. Be careful not to overcook the garlic at this stage or it will become bitter.

Add the courgettes, rosemary, parsley and lemon zest and juice. Cook for 3–4 minutes until the courgettes are just tender.

Add the olives to the frying pan and stir well. Season to taste with salt and pepper and remove from the heat.

Drain the pasta well and add to the frying pan. Stir until thoroughly combined. Garnish with lemon slices and sprigs of fresh rosemary and serve immediately.

Fusilli Pasta with Spicy Tomato Salsa

SERVES 2

3 large ripe tomatoes
1 tbsp lemon juice
1 tbsp lime juice
grated zest of 1 lime
2 shallots, peeled and

finely chopped
2 garlic cloves, peeled and
finely chopped
1–2 red chillies
1–2 green chillies

225 g/8 oz fresh fusilli pasta
2 tbsp crème fraîche
1 tbsp freshly chopped basil
oregano sprig, to garnish

Place the tomatoes in a bowl and cover with boiling water. Allow to stand until the skins start to peel away.

Remove the skins from the tomatoes, divide each tomato in four and remove all the seeds. Chop the flesh into small dice and put in a small pan. Add the lemon and lime juices and the grated lime zest and stir well.

Add the chopped shallots and garlic. Remove the seeds carefully from the chillies, chop finely and add to the pan. Bring to the boil and simmer gently for 5–10 minutes until the salsa has thickened slightly.

Reserve the salsa to allow the flavours to develop while the pasta is cooking.

Bring a large pan of water to the boil and add the pasta. Simmer gently for 3–4 minutes, or until the pasta is just tender.

Drain the pasta and rinse in boiling water. Top with a large spoonful of salsa and a spoonful of crème fraîche. Garnish with the chopped basil and oregano and serve immediately.

Spaghetti with Fresh Tomatoes, Chilli & Potatoes

SERVES 2

1 medium potato, unpeeled
1–2 garlic cloves, peeled and crushed
2 tbsp basil, roughly chopped
3 tbsp olive oil

2 large ripe plum tomatoes, skinned, deseeded and chopped
1 small red chilli, deseeded and finely chopped
salt and freshly ground

black pepper
225 g/8 oz spaghetti
2 tbsp freshly grated Parmesan cheese, to serve (optional)

Preheat the grill to high, 5 minutes before using. Cook the potato in plenty of boiling water until tender but firm. Allow to cool, then peel and cut into cubes.

Blend the garlic, basil and 2 tablespoons of the olive oil in a blender or food processor until the basil is finely chopped, then reserve.

Place the tomatoes and the basil and oil mixture in a small bowl, add the chilli and season with salt and pepper to taste. Mix together and reserve the sauce.

Bring a large pan of salted water to a rolling boil, add the spaghetti and cook according to the packet instructions, or until *al dente*.

Meanwhile, toss the potato cubes with the remaining olive oil and transfer to a baking sheet. Place the potatoes under the preheated grill until they are crisp and golden, turning once or twice, then drain on absorbent kitchen paper.

Drain the pasta thoroughly and transfer to a warmed shallow serving bowl. Add the tomato sauce and the hot potatoes. Toss well and adjust the seasoning to taste. Serve immediately with the grated Parmesan cheese, if using.

Spaghettini with Peas, Spring Onions & Mint

SERVES 2

pinch saffron strands
350 g/12 oz fresh peas or
175 g/6oz frozen petit
pois, thawed
40 g/1½ oz unsalted butter,
softened

3 spring onions, trimmed
and finely sliced
salt and freshly ground
black pepper
1 garlic clove, peeled and
finely chopped

1 tbsp freshly chopped mint
225 g/8 oz spaghettini
freshly grated Parmesan
cheese, to serve

Soak the saffron in 2 tablespoons hot water while you prepare the sauce. Shell the peas if using fresh ones.

Heat 25 g/1 oz of the butter in a medium frying pan, add the spring onions and a little salt and cook over a low heat for 2–3 minutes, or until the onions are softened. Add the garlic, then the peas and 50 ml/2 fl oz water. Bring to the boil and cook for 5–6 minutes, or until the peas are just tender. Stir in the mint and keep warm.

Blend the remaining butter and the saffron water in a large warmed serving bowl and reserve.

Meanwhile, bring a large pan of lightly salted water to a rolling boil and add the spaghettini. Cook according to the packet instructions, or until *al dente*.

Drain thoroughly, reserving 2–3 tablespoons of the pasta cooking water. Tip into a warmed serving bowl, add the pea sauce and toss together gently. Season to taste with salt and pepper. Serve immediately with extra black pepper and grated Parmesan cheese.

HELPFUL HINT

Saffron is one of the few spices that can be kept for several years, but you must store it in an airtight container, away from light.

Four-cheese Tagliatelle

SERVES 2

150 ml/¼ pint whipping cream
2 garlic cloves, peeled and lightly bruised
40 g/1½ oz fontina cheese, diced
40 g/1½ oz Gruyère cheese, grated
40 g/1½ oz mozzarella cheese, diced
25 g/1 oz Parmesan cheese, grated, plus extra to serve
salt and freshly ground black pepper
225 g/8 oz fresh green tagliatelle
1–2 tbsp freshly snipped chives
fresh basil leaves, to garnish

Place the whipping cream with the garlic cloves in a medium pan and heat gently until small bubbles begin to form around the edge of the pan. Using a slotted spoon, remove and discard the garlic cloves.

Add all the cheeses to the pan and stir until melted. Season with a little salt and plenty of black pepper. Keep the sauce warm over a low heat, but do not allow to boil.

Meanwhile, bring a large pan of lightly salted water to the boil. Add the tagliatelle, return to the boil and cook for 2–3 minutes, or until *al dente*.

Drain the pasta thoroughly and return to the pan. Pour the sauce over the pasta, add the chives then toss lightly until well coated. Tip into a warmed serving dish or spoon onto individual plates. Garnish with a few basil leaves and serve immediately with extra Parmesan cheese.

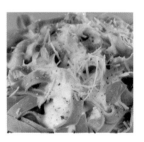

Spaghetti alla Puttanesca

SERVES 2

2 tbsp olive oil
25 g/1 oz anchovy fillets
　in olive oil, drained
　and coarsely chopped
2 garlic cloves, peeled and
　finely chopped
½ tsp crushed dried chillies

200 g/7 oz canned chopped
　plum tomatoes
50 g/2 oz pitted black olives,
　cut in half
1 tbsp capers, rinsed
　and drained
1 tsp freshly chopped

　oregano
2 tsp tomato purée
salt and freshly ground
　black pepper
200 g/7 oz spaghetti
1 tbsp freshly chopped
　parsley

Heat the olive oil in a large frying pan, add the anchovies and cook, stirring with a wooden spoon and crushing the anchovies, until they disintegrate. Add the garlic and dried chillies and cook for 1 minute, stirring frequently.

Add the tomatoes, olives, capers, oregano and tomato purée and cook, stirring occasionally, for 15 minutes, or until the liquid has evaporated and the sauce is thickened. Season the tomato sauce to taste with salt and pepper.

Meanwhile, bring a large pan of lightly salted water to a rolling boil. Add the spaghetti and cook according to the packet instructions, or until *al dente*.

Drain the spaghetti thoroughly, reserving 1–2 tablespoons of the cooking water. Return the spaghetti with the reserved water to the pan. Pour the tomato sauce over the spaghetti, add the chopped parsley and toss to coat. Tip into a warmed serving dish or spoon onto individual plates and serve immediately.

Rigatoni with Gorgonzola & Walnuts

SERVES 2

200 g/7 oz rigatoni
25 g/1 oz butter
50 g/2 oz crumbled
    Gorgonzola cheese
1 tbsp brandy (optional)
100 ml/3½ fl oz whipping or
    double cream

40 g/1½ oz walnut pieces,
    lightly toasted and
    coarsely chopped
1 tbsp freshly chopped basil
25 g/1 oz freshly grated
    Parmesan cheese
salt and freshly ground

black pepper

To serve:
cherry tomatoes
fresh green salad leaves

Bring a large pan of lightly salted water to a rolling boil. Add the rigatoni and cook according to the packet instructions, or until *al dente*. Drain the pasta thoroughly, reserve and keep warm.

Melt the butter in a saucepan over a medium heat. Add the Gorgonzola cheese and stir until just melted. Add the brandy if using and cook for 30 seconds, then pour in the cream and cook for 1–2 minutes, stirring, until the sauce is smooth.

Stir in the walnut pieces, basil and half the Parmesan cheese, then add the rigatoni. Season to taste with salt and pepper. Return to the heat, stirring frequently, until heated through.

Divide the pasta among two warmed pasta bowls, sprinkle with the remaining Parmesan cheese and serve immediately with cherry tomatoes and fresh green salad leaves.

Special Occasions

Seared Tuna with Pernod & Thyme

SERVES 2

2 tuna or swordfish steaks
salt and freshly ground
    black pepper
2 tbsp Pernod

1 tbsp olive oil
grated zest and juice of 1 lime
2 tsp fresh thyme leaves
4 sun-dried tomatoes

To serve:
freshly cooked mixed rice
tossed green salad

Wipe the fish steaks with a damp cloth or dampened kitchen paper.

Season both sides of the fish to taste with salt and pepper, then place in a shallow bowl and reserve.

Mix together the Pernod, olive oil, lime zest and juice with the fresh thyme leaves.

Finely chop the sun-dried tomatoes and add to the Pernod mixture.

Pour the Pernod mixture over the fish and chill in the refrigerator for about 2 hours, spooning the marinade occasionally over the fish.

Heat a griddle or heavy-based frying pan. Drain the fish, reserving the marinade. Cook the fish for 3–4 minutes on each side for a steak that is still slightly pink in the middle. Or, if liked, cook the fish for 1–2 minutes longer on each side if you prefer your fish cooked through.

Place the remaining marinade in a small saucepan and bring to the boil. Pour the marinade over the fish and serve immediately with the mixed rice and salad.

Salmon with Strawberry Sauce

SERVES 2

2 x 150 g/5 oz salmon fillets
15 g/½ oz butter
4 tsp olive or groundnut oil
1 small dessert apple, cored
  and cut into chunks
4 spring onions, trimmed
  and diagonally sliced

1 garlic clove, peeled
  and sliced
25 g/1 oz pine nuts
juice of 1 lemon
50 g/2 oz strawberries,
  hulled and halved
1 tbsp basil, freshly chopped

salt and freshly ground
  black pepper

To serve:
freshly cooked creamy
  mashed potatoes
freshly cooked broad beans

Lightly rinse the salmon fillets and pat dry on absorbent kitchen paper. Heat the wok, then add the butter and half the oil and heat until bubbling. Cook the salmon fillets flesh-side down for 5 minutes until they are sealed. Then, using a fish slice, carefully turn the salmon fillets over and cook for a further 3–5 minutes until the salmon flesh is just flaking.

Transfer the salmon fillets to warmed serving plates and keep warm in a low oven. Wipe the wok clean, then add the remaining oil to the wok and heat until almost smoking.

Add the apple chunks, spring onions, garlic slices and pine nuts and cook for 5 minutes, stirring occasionally, until they are golden brown.

Stir in the lemon juice, strawberries and chopped basil and season to taste with salt and pepper. Heat through thoroughly.

Spoon the sauce over the salmon fillets and serve immediately with creamy mashed potatoes and freshly cooked broad beans.

Spaghetti with Smoked Salmon & Tiger Prawns

SERVES 2

125 g/4 oz baby spinach leaves
salt and freshly ground black pepper
pinch freshly grated nutmeg
125 g/4 oz cooked tiger prawns in their shells

225 g/8 oz fresh angel hair spaghetti
25 g/1 oz butter
2 small eggs
1 tbsp freshly chopped dill, plus extra to garnish
75 g/3 oz smoked salmon,

cut into strips
dill sprigs, to garnish
1 tbsp grated Parmesan cheese, to serve

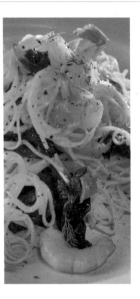

Cook the baby spinach leaves in a large pan with 1 teaspoon of water for 3–4 minutes, or until wilted. Drain thoroughly, season to taste with salt, pepper and nutmeg and keep warm. Remove the shells from all but 4 of the tiger prawns and reserve.

Bring a large pan of lightly salted water to a rolling boil. Add the pasta and cook according to the packet instructions, about 3–4 minutes, or until *al dente*. Drain thoroughly and return to the pan. Stir in the butter and the peeled prawns, cover and keep warm.

Beat the eggs with the dill, season well, then stir into the pasta and prawns. Return the pan to the heat briefly, just long enough to lightly scramble the eggs, then remove from the heat. Carefully mix in the smoked salmon strips and the cooked spinach. Toss gently to mix.

Tip into a warmed serving dish and garnish with the reserved prawns and dill sprigs.

Serve immediately with grated Parmesan cheese.

HELPFUL HINT

Make sure that you use cooked and not raw prawns. If you buy them raw, remove the heads and shells then briefly sauté in a little olive oil until just pink and opaque.

Farfalle with Smoked Trout in a Dill & Vodka Sauce

SERVES 2

200 g/7 oz farfalle
75 g/3 oz smoked trout
2 tsp lemon juice
100 ml/3½ oz double cream

1 tsp wholegrain mustard
1 tbsp freshly chopped dill
2 tbsp vodka
salt and freshly ground

black pepper
dill sprigs, to garnish

Bring a large pan of lightly salted water to a rolling boil. Add the pasta and cook according to the packet instructions, or until *al dente*.

Meanwhile, cut the smoked trout into thin slivers, using scissors. Sprinkle lightly with the lemon juice and reserve.

Place the cream, mustard, chopped dill and vodka in a small pan. Season lightly with salt and pepper. Bring the contents of the pan to the boil and simmer gently for 2–3 minutes, or until slightly thickened.

Drain the cooked pasta thoroughly, then return to the pan. Add the smoked trout to the dill and vodka sauce, then pour over the pasta. Toss gently until the pasta is coated and the trout evenly mixed.

Spoon into a warmed serving dish or onto individual plates. Garnish with sprigs of dill and serve immediately.

Sole with Red Wine Sauce

SERVES 2

2 tbsp sunflower or
   groundnut oil
50 g/2 oz unsmoked streaky
   bacon, rind removed,
   and diced
75 g/3 oz shallots, peeled
   and chopped
125 g/4 oz button
   mushrooms, wiped

1 tbsp plain flour
1 tbsp brandy,
150 ml/¼ pint red wine
1 bouquet garni
1 garlic clove, peeled and
   chopped
salt and freshly ground
   black pepper
4 sole fillets, skinned and

   cut in half
fresh parsley sprigs,
   to garnish

To serve:
freshly cooked noodles
mangetout

Heat a frying pan or wok, add the oil and heat. When hot, stir-fry the bacon and shallots for 4–5 minutes, or until golden. Using a slotted spoon, remove from the wok and keep warm. Add the mushrooms and stir-fry for 2 minutes, then remove and reserve.

Sprinkle the flour into the pan and carefully stir-fry over a medium heat for 30 seconds. Remove from the heat, then return the bacon and shallots to the pan together with the brandy.

Stir in the red wine, bouquet garni and garlic and season to taste with salt and pepper. Return to the heat and bring back to the boil, stirring until smooth, then simmer for about 5 minutes until the sauce has thickened.

Meanwhile, roll the sole fillets up and secure with either fine twine or cocktail sticks. Carefully add the rolled-up sole fillets and reserved mushrooms with seasoning to the pan. Reduce the heat, cover with a lid or kitchen foil and simmer for a further 8–10 minutes, or until the fish is tender. Discard the bouquet garni, garnish with sprigs of fresh parsley and serve immediately with freshly cooked noodles and steamed mangetout.

Thai Green Fragrant Mussels

SERVES 2

1 kg/2.2 lb fresh mussels
2 tbsp olive oil
1 garlic clove, peeled and
    finely sliced
1 tbsp fresh root ginger,
    peeled and finely sliced
1 lemon grass stalk, outer
    leaves discarded, and

finely sliced
1–2 red or green chillies,
    deseeded and chopped
1 small green pepper,
    deseeded and diced
3 spring onions, trimmed
    and finely sliced
1–2 tbsp freshly chopped

coriander
1 tsp sesame oil
juice of 1 lime
200 ml/7 fl oz canned
    coconut milk
warm crusty bread, to serve

Scrub the mussels under cold running water, removing any barnacles and beards. Discard any that have broken or damaged shells or are opened and do not close when tapped gently.

Heat a wok or large frying pan, add the oil and, when hot, add the mussels. Shake gently and cook for 1 minute, then add the garlic, ginger, sliced lemon grass, chillies, green pepper, spring onions, half the chopped coriander, or to taste, and the sesame oil.

Stir-fry over a medium heat for 3–4 minutes, or until the mussels are cooked and have opened. Discard any mussels that remain unopened.

Pour the lime juice with the coconut milk into the wok and bring to the boil. Tip the mussels and the cooking liquor into warmed individual bowls. Sprinkle with the remaining chopped coriander and serve immediately with warm crusty bread.

HELPFUL HINT

If overcooked, mussels will toughen and lose their fresh sea flavour. Add the lime juice and coconut milk as soon as they have opened and quickly bring to the boil.

Scallop & Potato Gratin

4 fresh scallops in their
shells, cleaned
2 tbsp white wine
salt and freshly ground
black pepper

25 g/1 oz butter
15 g/½ oz plain flour
1 tbsp single cream
25 g/1 oz Cheddar cheese,
grated

225 g/8 oz potatoes, peeled
and cut into chunks
1 tbsp milk

Preheat the oven to 220°C/425°F/Gas Mark 7. Clean 2 scallop shells to use as serving dishes and reserve. Place the scallops in a small saucepan with the wine, 85 ml/3 fl oz water and salt and pepper. Cover and simmer very gently for 5 minutes, or until just tender. Remove with a slotted spoon and cut each scallop into 3 pieces. Reserve the cooking juices.

Melt half the butter in a saucepan, stir in the flour and cook for 1 minute, stirring, then gradually whisk in the reserved cooking juices. Simmer, stirring, for 3–4 minutes until the sauce has thickened. Season to taste with salt and pepper. Remove from the heat and stir in the cream and half the grated cheese. Fold in the scallops.

Meanwhile, boil the potatoes in lightly salted water until tender, then mash with the remaining butter and the milk. Spoon or pipe the mashed potato around the edges of the cleaned scallop shells.

Divide the scallop mixture between the 2 shells, placing the mixture neatly in the centre. Sprinkle with the remaining grated cheese and bake in the preheated oven for about 10–15 minutes until golden brown and bubbling. Serve immediately.

HELPFUL HINT

The simplest and safest way to open scallops is to place them flat-side up on a baking sheet and put in a hot oven for a few minutes. Prise open and remove the meat.

Penne with Vodka & Caviar

SERVES 2

200 g/7 oz penne
15 g/½ oz butter
2–3 spring onions, trimmed
    and thinly sliced
1 garlic clove, peeled and

finely chopped
50 ml/2 fl oz vodka
125 ml/4 fl oz double cream
1 ripe plum tomato, skinned,
    deseeded and chopped

40 g/1½ oz caviar
salt and freshly ground
    black pepper

Bring a large pan of lightly salted water to a rolling boil. Add the penne and cook according to the packet instructions, or until *al dente*. Drain thoroughly and reserve.

Heat the butter in a large frying pan or wok, add the spring onions and stir-fry for 1 minute. Stir in the garlic and cook for a further 1 minute. Pour the vodka into the pan; it will bubble and steam. Cook until the vodka is reduced by about half, then add the double cream and return to the boil. Simmer gently for 2–3 minutes, or until the sauce has thickened slightly.

Stir in the chopped tomato, then stir in all but half a tablespoon of the caviar and season to taste with salt and pepper. Add the penne and toss lightly to coat. Cook for 1 minute, or until heated through. Divide the mixture among 2 warmed pasta bowls and garnish with the reserved caviar. Serve immediately.

Conchiglioni with Crab au Gratin

SERVES 2

125 g/4 oz large pasta shells
25 g/1 oz butter
1 shallot, peeled and
    finely chopped
1 bird's-eye chilli, deseeded
    and finely chopped
200 g/7 oz can crab meat,
    drained

2 tbsp plain flour
25 ml/1 fl oz white wine
25 ml/1 fl oz milk
2 tbsp crème fraîche
15 g/½ oz Cheddar cheese,
    grated
salt and freshly ground
    black pepper

25 g/1 oz fresh white
    breadcrumbs
1 tbsp oil or melted butter

To serve:
cheese or tomato sauce
tossed green salad or freshly
    cooked baby vegetables

Preheat the oven to 200°C/400°F/Gas Mark 6, 15 minutes before cooking. Bring a large pan of lightly salted water to a rolling boil. Add the pasta shells and cook according to the packet instructions, or until *al dente*. Drain thoroughly and allow to dry completely.

Melt half the butter in a heavy-based pan, add the shallot and chilli and cook for 2 minutes, then stir in the crab meat. Stuff the cooled shells with the crab mixture and reserve.

Melt the remaining butter in a small pan and stir in the flour. Cook for 1 minute, then whisk in the wine and milk and cook, stirring, until thickened. Stir in the crème fraîche and grated cheese and season the sauce to taste with salt and pepper.

Place the crab-filled shells in a lightly oiled shallow baking dish or tray and spoon a little of the sauce over. Toss the breadcrumbs in the oil or melted butter, then sprinkle over the pasta shells. Bake in the preheated oven for 10 minutes. Serve immediately with a cheese or tomato sauce and a tossed green salad or cooked baby vegetables.

Fillet Steaks with Tomato & Garlic Sauce

SERVES 2

350 g/12 oz ripe tomatoes
1–2 garlic cloves
1 tbsp olive oil
1 tbsp freshly chopped basil
1 tbsp freshly chopped

oregano
2 tbsp red wine
salt and freshly ground
  black pepper
40 g/1½ oz pitted black

olives, chopped
2 fillet steaks, about 150 g/5
  oz each in weight
freshly cooked vegetables,
  to serve

Make a small cross on the top of each tomato and place in a large bowl. Cover with boiling water and leave for 2 minutes. Using a slotted spoon, remove the tomatoes and skin carefully. Repeat until all the tomatoes are skinned. Place on a chopping board, cut into quarters, remove the seeds and chop roughly, then reserve.

Peel and chop the garlic. Heat half the olive oil in a saucepan and cook the garlic for 30 seconds. Add the chopped tomatoes with the basil, oregano and red wine and season to taste with salt and pepper. Bring to the boil, then reduce the heat, cover and simmer for 15 minutes, stirring occasionally, or until the sauce is reduced and thickened. Stir the olives into the sauce and keep warm while cooking the steaks.

Meanwhile, lightly oil a griddle pan or heavy-based frying pan with the remaining olive oil and cook the steaks for 2 minutes on each side to seal. Continue to cook the steaks for a further 2–4 minutes, depending on personal preference. Serve the steaks immediately with the garlic sauce and freshly cooked vegetables.

Fettuccine with Calves' Liver & Calvados

SERVES 2

225 g/8 oz calves' liver, trimmed and thinly sliced
25 g/1 oz plain flour
salt and freshly ground black pepper

1 tsp paprika
25 g/1 oz butter
1 tbsp olive oil
2 tbsp Calvados
75 ml/3 fl oz cider

75 ml/3 fl oz whipping cream
175 g/6 oz fresh fettuccine
fresh thyme sprigs, to garnish

Season the flour with the salt, black pepper and paprika, then toss the liver in the flour until well coated.

Melt half the butter and half the olive oil in a large frying pan and fry the liver for 1 minute, or until just browned but still slightly pink inside. Remove using a slotted spoon and place in a warmed dish.

Add the remaining butter to the pan, stir in 1 tablespoon of the seasoned flour and cook for 1 minute. Pour in the Calvados and cider and cook over a high heat for 30 seconds. Stir the cream into the sauce and simmer for 1 minute to thicken slightly, then season to taste. Return the liver to the pan and heat through.

Bring a large pan of lightly salted water to a rolling boil. Add the fettuccine and cook according to the packet instructions, about 3–4 minutes, or until *al dente.*

Drain the fettuccine thoroughly, return to the pan and toss in the remaining olive oil. Place on two warmed plates and spoon the liver and sauce over the pasta. Garnish with thyme sprigs and serve immediately.

Pork with Tofu

SERVES 2

175 g/6 oz smoked firm tofu, drained
1 tbsp sunflower or groundnut oil
1–2 garlic cloves, peeled and crushed
1 cm/½ inch piece fresh root ginger, peeled and finely chopped
175 g/6 oz fresh pork mince
2 tsp chilli powder
1 tsp sugar
1 tbsp Chinese rice wine
1 tsp dark soy sauce
1 tsp light soy sauce
1 tbsp yellow bean sauce
1 tsp Szechuan peppercorns
50 ml/2 fl oz chicken stock
1 spring onion, trimmed and finely sliced, to garnish
fried rice, to serve

Cut the tofu into 1 cm/½ inch cubes and place in a sieve to drain. Place the tofu on absorbent kitchen paper to dry thoroughly for 10 minutes.

Heat a frying pan or wok, add the oil and, when hot, add the garlic and ginger. Stir-fry for a few seconds to flavour the oil, but not to colour the vegetables. Add the pork mince and stir-fry for 3 minutes, or until the pork is sealed and there are no lumps in the mince.

Add all the remaining ingredients except the tofu. Bring the mixture to the boil, then reduce the heat to low. Add the tofu and mix it in gently, taking care not to break it up but ensuring an even mixture of ingredients. Simmer, uncovered, for 15 minutes, or until the tofu is tender. Turn into a warmed serving dish, garnish with sliced spring onions and serve immediately with fried rice.

Cannelloni with Gorgonzola Sauce

SERVES 2

25 g/1 oz salted butter
1 shallot, peeled and finely
    chopped
2 rashers streaky bacon, rind
    removed, and chopped
175 g/6 oz mushrooms,

wiped and finely chopped
25 g/1 oz plain flour
125 ml/4 fl oz double cream
125 g/4 oz fresh egg lasagne,
    6 sheets in total
40 g/1½ oz unsalted butter

150 g/5 oz Gorgonzola
    cheese, diced
150 ml/¼ pint whipping cream
assorted salad leaves,
    to serve

Preheat the oven to 190°C/375°F/Gas Mark 5, 10 minutes before cooking. Melt the salted butter in a heavy-based pan, add the shallot and bacon and cook for about 4–5 minutes.

Add the mushrooms to the pan and cook for 5–6 minutes, or until the mushrooms are very soft. Stir in the flour, cook for 1 minute, then stir in the double cream and cook gently for 2 minutes. Allow to cool.

Cut each sheet of lasagne in half. Spoon some filling onto each piece and roll up from the longest side to resemble cannelloni. Arrange the cannelloni in a lightly oiled shallow 1.4 litre/2½ pint ovenproof dish.

Heat the unsalted butter very slowly in a pan and, when melted, add the Gorgonzola cheese. Stir until the cheese has melted, then stir in the whipping cream. Bring to the boil slowly, then simmer gently for about 5 minutes, or until thickened.

Pour the cream sauce over the cannelloni. Place in the preheated oven and bake for 20 minutes, or until golden and thoroughly heated through. Serve immediately with assorted salad leaves.

Kung–pao Lamb

225 g/8 oz lamb fillet
1 tbsp soy sauce
1 tbsp Chinese rice wine
    or dry sherry
1 tbsp sunflower oil
2 tsp sesame oil
50 g/2 oz unsalted peanuts
1 garlic clove, peeled and

crushed
1 cm/½ inch piece fresh root
    ginger, finely chopped
1 red chilli, deseeded and
    finely chopped
1 small green pepper,
    deseeded and diced
3 spring onions, trimmed

and diagonally sliced
50 ml/2 fl oz lamb or
    vegetable stock
1 tsp red wine vinegar
1 tsp soft light brown sugar
2 tsp cornflour
plain boiled or steamed
    white rice, to serve

Wrap the lamb in baking parchment and place in the freezer for about 30 minutes until stiff. Cut the meat across the grain into paper-thin slices. Put in a shallow bowl, add 2 teaspoons of the soy sauce and all the Chinese rice wine or sherry and leave to marinate in the refrigerator for 15 minutes.

Heat a frying pan or wok until hot, add the sunflower oil and swirl it around to coat the sides. Add the lamb and stir-fry for about 1 minute until lightly browned. Remove from the pan and reserve, leaving any juices behind.

Add the sesame oil to the pan and stir-fry the peanuts, garlic, ginger, chilli, green pepper and spring onions for 1–2 minutes, or until the nuts are golden. Return the lamb with the remaining soy sauce, stock, vinegar and sugar.

Blend the cornflour with 1 tablespoon of water. Stir in and cook the mixture for 1–2 minutes, or until the vegetables are tender and the sauce has thickened. Serve immediately with plain boiled or steamed white rice.

Creamy Chicken Stroganoff

SERVES 2

225 g/8 oz skinless chicken breast fillets
2 tbsp dry sherry
15 g/½ oz dried porcini mushrooms
1 tbsp sunflower oil
25 g/1 oz unsalted butter
1 small onion, peeled and sliced

125 g/4 oz chestnut mushrooms, wiped and sliced
1 tsp paprika
1 tsp freshly chopped thyme
50 ml/2 fl oz chicken stock
75 ml/3 fl oz crème fraîche
salt and freshly ground black pepper

sprigs of fresh thyme, to garnish

To serve:
crème fraîche
freshly cooked rice or egg noodles

Cut the chicken into finger-length strips and reserve. Gently warm the sherry in a small saucepan and remove from the heat. Add the porcini mushrooms and leave to soak while preparing the rest of the stir-fried ingredients.

Heat a frying pan or wok, add half the oil and, when hot, add the chicken and stir-fry over a high heat for 3–4 minutes, or until lightly browned, remove and reserve.

Wipe the pan clean, then heat the remaining oil and butter. Gently cook the onion for 5 minutes. Add the chestnut mushrooms and stir-fry for a further 5 minutes, or until tender. Sprinkle in the paprika and thyme and cook for 30 seconds.

Add the porcini mushrooms with their soaking liquid, then stir in the stock and return the chicken to the pan. Cook for 1–2 minutes, or until the chicken is cooked through and tender.

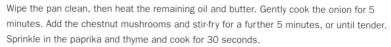

Stir in the crème fraîche and heat until piping hot. Season to taste with salt and pepper. Garnish with sprigs of fresh thyme and serve immediately with a spoonful of crème fraîche and rice or egg noodles.

Spatchcocked Poussins with Garlic Sage Butter

SERVES 2

For the herb butter:
3 garlic cloves
50 g/2 oz butter, softened
1 tbsp freshly snipped
   chives
1 tbsp freshly chopped sage
grated zest and juice of 1

small lemon
salt and freshly ground
   black pepper

For the poussins:
2 spatchcocked poussins
2 tbsp extra-virgin olive oil

To garnish:
chives
fresh sage leaves

To serve:
grilled polenta
grilled tomatoes

Preheat the grill or light an outdoor charcoal grill and line the grill rack with kitchen foil, just before cooking. Put the garlic cloves in a small saucepan and cover with cold water. Bring to the boil, then simmer for 5 minutes, or until softened. Drain and cool slightly. Cut off the root end of each clove and squeeze the softened garlic into a bowl. Pound the garlic until smooth, then beat in the butter, chives, sage and lemon zest and juice. Season to taste with salt and pepper.

Using your fingertips, gently loosen the skin from each poussin breast by sliding your hand between the skin and the flesh. Push one half of the herb butter under the skin, spreading evenly over the breast and the top of the thighs. Pull the neck skin gently to tighten the skin over the breast and tuck under the bird. Repeat with the remaining poussin and herb butter.

Thread two wooden skewers crossways through each poussin, from one wing through the opposite leg, to keep the poussin flat. Brush with the olive oil and season with salt and pepper. Arrange the poussins on the foil-lined rack and grill for 25 minutes, turning occasionally, until golden and crisp and the juices run clear when a thigh is pierced with a sharp knife or skewer. (Position the rack about 12.5 cm/5 inches from the heat source or the skin will brown before the birds are cooked through.) Garnish with chives and sage leaves and serve immediately with grilled polenta and a few grilled tomatoes.

Guinea Fowl with Calvados & Apples

SERVES 2

2 guinea fowl supremes, each about 150 g/5 oz, skinned
2 tsp plain flour
1 tbsp sunflower oil
1 small onion, peeled and finely sliced
1 garlic clove, peeled

and crushed
1 tsp freshly chopped thyme
75 ml/3 fl oz dry cider
salt and freshly ground black pepper
2 tbsp Calvados brandy
sprigs of fresh thyme, to garnish

For the carmelised apples:
15 g/½ oz unsalted butter
1 red-skinned eating apple, quartered, cored and sliced
1 tsp caster sugar

Lightly dust the guinea fowl supremes with the flour. Heat 2 teaspoons of the oil in a large nonstick frying pan and cook the supremes for 2–3 minutes on each side until browned. Remove from the pan and reserve.

Heat the remaining teaspoon of oil in the pan and add the onion and garlic. Cook over a medium heat for 5–8 minutes, stirring occasionally, until soft and just beginning to colour. Stir in the chopped thyme and cider. Return the guinea fowl to the pan, season with salt and pepper and bring to a very gentle simmer. Cover and cook over a low heat for 15–20 minutes, or until the guinea fowl is tender. Remove the guinea fowl and keep warm. Turn up the heat and boil the sauce until thickened and reduced by half.

Meanwhile, prepare the caramelised apple. Melt the butter in a small nonstick pan, add the apple slices in a single layer and sprinkle with the sugar. Cook until the apples are tender and beginning to caramelise, turning once. Put the Calvados in a metal ladle or small saucepan and gently heat until warm. Carefully set alight with a match, let the flames die down, then stir into the sauce.

Serve the guinea fowl with the sauce spooned over and garnished with the caramelised apple and sprigs of fresh thyme.

Pheasant with Sage & Blueberries

SERVES 2

1 tbsp olive oil
2 shallots, peeled and
  coarsely chopped
2 fresh sage sprigs, coarsely
  chopped
1 bay leaf
1 lemon, halved

salt and freshly ground
  black pepper
1 pheasant or guinea fowl,
  rinsed and dried
50 g/2 oz blueberries
2 slices Parma ham or bacon
50 ml/2 fl oz vermouth or dry

white wine
100 ml/3½ fl oz chicken stock
2 tbsp double cream or
  butter (optional)
1 tbsp brandy
roast potatoes, to serve

Preheat the oven to 180°C/350°F/Gas Mark 4, 10 minutes before cooking. Place the oil, shallots, sage and bay leaf in a bowl with the juice from the lemon halves. Season with salt and pepper. Tuck the squeezed lemon halves into the pheasant body cavity with 40 g/1½ oz of the blueberries, then rub the pheasant with the marinade and leave for 2–3 hours, basting occasionally.

Remove the pheasant from the marinade and cover with the slices of Parma ham or bacon. Tie the legs of the pheasant with string and place in a roasting tin. Pour over the marinade and add the vermouth or wine. Roast in the preheated oven for 1 hour, or until tender and golden and the juices run clear when a thigh is pierced with a sharp knife or skewer. Transfer to a warm serving plate, discard the string and cover the pheasant with kitchen foil. Skim off any surface fat from the tin and set over a medium-high heat.

Add the stock to the tin and bring to the boil, scraping any browned bits from the bottom. Boil until slightly reduced. Whisk in the cream or butter, if using, and simmer until thickened, whisking constantly. Stir in the brandy and strain into a gravy jug. Add the remaining blueberries and keep warm.

Using a sharp carving knife, cut the pheasant in half and arrange on the plate with the crispy Parma ham. Serve immediately with roast potatoes and the gravy.

Duck with Berry Sauce

SERVES 2

2 x 175 g/6 oz boneless
   duck breasts
salt and freshly ground
   black pepper
1 tsp sunflower oil

For the sauce:
juice of 1 small orange

1 bay leaf
1 tbsp redcurrant jelly
75 g/3 oz fresh or frozen
   mixed berries
1 tbsp dried cranberries or
   cherries
½ tsp soft light brown sugar
1 tsp balsamic vinegar

1 tsp freshly chopped mint
fresh mint sprigs,
   to garnish

To serve:
freshly cooked potatoes
freshly cooked green beans

Remove the skins from the duck breasts and season with a little salt and pepper. Brush a griddle pan with the oil, then heat on the stove until smoking hot.

Place the duck skinned-side down in the pan. Cook over a medium-high heat for 5 minutes, or until well browned. Turn the duck and cook for 2 minutes. Lower the heat and cook for a further 5–8 minutes, or until cooked but still slightly pink in the centre. Remove from the pan and keep warm.

While the duck is cooking, make the sauce. Put the orange juice, bay leaf, redcurrant jelly, fresh or frozen and dried berries and sugar in a small pan. Add any juices left in the griddle pan to the small pan. Slowly bring to the boil, lower the heat and simmer, uncovered, for 4–5 minutes until the fruit is soft.

Remove the bay leaf. Stir in the vinegar and chopped mint and season to taste with salt and pepper.

Slice the duck breasts on the diagonal and arrange on serving plates. Spoon over the berry sauce and garnish with sprigs of fresh mint. Serve immediately with the potatoes and green beans.

Warm Potato, Pear & Pecan Salad

SERVES 2

450 g /1 lb new potatoes, preferably red-skinned, unpeeled
1 tsp Dijon mustard
1 tsp white wine vinegar

2 tbsp groundnut oil
1 tbsp hazelnut or walnut oil
1 tsp poppy seeds
salt and freshly ground black pepper

1 firm ripe dessert pear
2 tsp lemon juice
75 g/3 oz baby spinach leaves
40 g/1½ oz toasted pecan nuts

Scrub the potatoes, then cook in a saucepan of lightly salted boiling water for 15 minutes, or until tender. Drain, cut into halves, or quarters if large, and place in a serving bowl.

In a small bowl or jug, whisk together the mustard and vinegar. Gradually add the oils until the mixture begins to thicken. Stir in the poppy seeds and season to taste with salt and pepper.

Pour about two-thirds of the dressing over the hot potatoes and toss gently to coat. Leave until the potatoes have soaked up the dressing and are just warm.

Meanwhile, quarter and core the pear. Cut into thin slices, then sprinkle with the lemon juice to prevent them from going brown. Add to the potatoes with the spinach leaves and toasted pecan nuts. Gently mix together.

Drizzle the remaining dressing over the salad. Serve immediately, before the spinach starts to wilt.

HELPFUL HINT

To toast the nuts, bake in a single layer in a preheated oven at 180°C/350°F/Gas Mark 4 for 5 minutes, or under a medium grill for 3–4 minutes, turning frequently. Be careful – they burn easily.

Aubergine Cannelloni with Watercress Sauce

SERVES 2

2 aubergines, about 250 g/9 oz each
3–4 tbsp olive oil
175 g/6 oz ricotta cheese
40 g/1½ oz Parmesan cheese, grated
2 tbsp freshly chopped basil
salt and freshly ground black pepper

For the watercress sauce:
40 g/1½ oz watercress, trimmed
100 ml/3½ fl oz vegetable stock
1 shallot, peeled and sliced
pared strip of lemon zest
1 thyme sprig
2 tbsp crème fraîche
1 tsp lemon juice

To garnish:
watercress sprigs
lemon zest strands

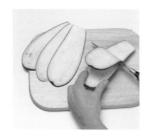

Preheat the oven to 190°C/375°F/Gas Mark 5, 10 minutes before cooking. Cut the aubergines lengthways into thin slices, discarding the side pieces. Heat 2 tablespoons of oil in a frying pan and cook the aubergine slices in a single layer in several batches, turning once, until golden on both sides. Add more oil as required.

Mix the cheeses, basil and seasoning together. Lay the aubergine slices on a clean surface and spread the cheese mixture evenly between them. Roll up the slices from one of the short ends to enclose the filling. Place seam-side down in a single layer in an ovenproof dish. Bake in the preheated oven for 15 minutes, or until golden.

To make the watercress sauce, blanch the watercress leaves in boiling water for about 30 seconds. Drain well, then rinse in a sieve under cold running water and squeeze dry. Put the stock, shallot, lemon zest and thyme in a small saucepan. Boil rapidly until reduced by half, then remove from the heat and strain. Put the watercress and strained stock in a food processor and blend until fairly smooth. Return to the saucepan and stir in the crème fraîche, lemon juice and season to taste with salt and pepper. Heat gently until the sauce is piping hot.

Serve a little of the sauce drizzled over the aubergines and the rest separately in a jug. Garnish with sprigs of watercress and the strands of lemon zest. Serve immediately.

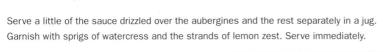

Wild Mushroom Risotto

SERVES 2

15 g/½ oz dried porcini
600 ml/1 pt vegetable stock
40 g/1½ oz butter
1 tbsp olive oil
1 medium onion, peeled
    and chopped
1–2 garlic cloves, peeled
    and chopped
1–2 red chillies, deseeded

and chopped
125 g/4 oz wild mushrooms,
    wiped, and halved if large
125 g/4 oz button
    mushrooms, wiped
    and sliced
175 g/6 oz Arborio rice
75 g/3 oz large cooked
    prawns, peeled

75 ml/3 fl oz white wine
salt and freshly ground
    black pepper
1 tbsp grated lemon zest
1 tbsp freshly snipped chives
1 tbsp freshly chopped
    parsley

Soak the porcini in 150 ml/¼ pint very hot, but not boiling water for 30 minutes. Drain, reserving the mushrooms and soaking liquid. Pour the stock into a saucepan and bring to the boil, then reduce the heat to keep it simmering.

Melt the butter and oil in a large deep frying pan, add the onion, garlic and chillies and cook gently for 5 minutes. Add the wild and button mushrooms with the drained porcini and continue to cook for 4–5 minutes, stirring frequently.

Stir in the rice and cook for 1 minute. Strain the reserved soaking liquid and stir into the rice with a little of the hot stock. Cook gently, stirring frequently, until the liquid is absorbed. Continue to add most of the stock, a ladleful at a time, cooking after each addition, until the rice is tender and the risotto looks creamy.

Add the prawns and wine along with the last additions of stock. When the prawns are hot and all the liquid is absorbed, season to taste with salt and pepper. Remove from the heat and stir in the grated lemon zest, chives and parsley, reserving some for the garnish. Garnish and serve.

Pasta Triangles with Pesto & Walnut Dressing

SERVES 2

175 g/6 oz fresh egg lasagne
1½ tbsp ricotta cheese
1–2 tbsp, depending on taste, pesto
40 g/1½ oz walnuts
1 slice white bread, crusts removed

4 tbsp soured cream
25 g/1 oz mascarpone cheese
1–2 tbsp pecorino cheese, grated
salt and freshly ground black pepper
1 tbsp olive oil

dill sprig or freshly chopped basil or parsley, to garnish
tomato and cucumber salad, to serve

Preheat the grill to high. Cut the lasagne sheets in half, then into triangles and reserve. Mix the pesto and ricotta cheese together and warm gently in a pan.

Toast the walnuts under the preheated grill until golden. Rub off the papery skins. Place the nuts in a food processor with the bread and grind finely.

Mix the soured cream with the mascarpone cheese in a bowl. Add the ground walnuts and grated pecorino cheese and season to taste with salt and pepper. Whisk in the olive oil. Pour into a pan and warm gently.

Bring a large pan of lightly salted water to a rolling boil. Add the pasta triangles and cook, according to the packet instructions, about 3–4 minutes, or until *al dente*.

Drain the pasta thoroughly and arrange a few triangles on each serving plate. Top each one with a spoonful of the pesto mixture, then place another triangle on top. Continue to layer the pasta and pesto mixture, then spoon a little of the walnut sauce on top of each stack. Garnish with dill, basil or parsley and serve immediately with a freshly dressed tomato and cucumber salad.

Tagliatelle with Brown Butter, Asparagus & Parmesan

SERVES 2

175 g/6 oz asparagus, trimmed and cut into short lengths
40 g/1½ oz unsalted butter
1 garlic clove, peeled and sliced
15 g/½ oz flaked hazelnuts or whole hazelnuts, roughly chopped
1 tbsp freshly chopped parsley
1 tbsp freshly snipped chives
225 g/8 oz dried tagliatelle, such as the white and green variety
salt and freshly ground black pepper
25 g/1 oz freshly grated Parmesan cheese, to serve

Bring a pan of lightly salted water to the boil. Add the asparagus and cook for 1 minute. Drain immediately, refresh under cold running water and drain again. Pat dry and reserve.

Melt the butter in a large frying pan, then add the garlic and hazelnuts and cook over a medium heat until the butter turns golden. Immediately remove from the heat and add the parsley, chives and asparagus. Leave for 2–3 minutes until the asparagus is heated through.

Meanwhile, bring a large pan of lightly salted water to a rolling boil, then add the pasta. Cook until *al dente*: 2–3 minutes for fresh pasta and according to the packet instructions for dried pasta. Drain the pasta thoroughly and return to the pan. Add the asparagus mixture and toss together. Season to taste with salt and pepper and tip into a warmed serving dish. Serve immediately with grated Parmesan cheese.

HELPFUL HINT

It is best to buy asparagus no more than a day before using but, if you need to, you can keep stems fresh by standing them in a little water.

Cooking Ahead

Fish Lasagne

75 g/3 oz mushrooms
1 tsp sunflower oil
1 small onion, peeled
and finely chopped
1 tbsp freshly chopped
oregano
400 g/7 oz can chopped
tomatoes
1 tbsp tomato purée

salt and freshly ground
black pepper
450 g/1 lb fresh cod or
haddock fillets, skinned
9–12 sheets precooked
lasagne verde

For the topping:
1 medium egg, beaten

125 g/4 oz cottage cheese
150 ml/¼ pint natural yogurt
50 g/2 oz Cheddar
cheese, grated

To serve:
mixed salad leaves
cherry tomatoes

Preheat the oven to 190°C/375°F/Gas Mark 5. Wipe the mushrooms, trim the stalks and chop. Heat the oil in a large heavy-based pan, add the onion and cook gently for 3–5 minutes, or until soft. Stir in the mushrooms, the oregano and the chopped tomatoes with their juice. Blend the tomato purée with 1 tablespoon water. Stir into the pan and season to taste with salt and pepper. Bring the sauce to the boil, then simmer uncovered for 5–10 minutes.

Remove as many of the tiny pin bones as possible from the fish, cut into cubes and add to the tomato sauce mixture. Stir gently and remove the pan from the heat.

Cover the base of two small (600 ml/1 pint) ovenproof dishes with 1–2 sheets of the lasagne verde. If necessary, break the sheets to fit the dishes. Top with half the fish mixture. Repeat the layers, finishing with the lasagne sheets.

HELPFUL HINT

If your freezer contains a few delicious ready-made meals it is such a bonus when time is precious. So get ahead and make double the amount then freeze half – perfect.

To make the topping, mix together the beaten egg, cottage cheese and yogurt. Pour over the two lasagnes and sprinkle with the cheese. Wrap, label and date one lasagne and place in the freezer. Place the remaining lasagne on a baking tray and cook in the preheated oven for 30–35 minutes, or until the topping is golden brown and bubbling. Serve the lasagne immediately with the mixed salad leaves and cherry tomatoes.

Tuna Cannelloni

**SERVES 2 + 1 DISH
FOR FREEZING**

1 tbsp olive oil
6 spring onions, trimmed
    and finely sliced
1 sweet Mediterranean
    red pepper, deseeded
    and finely chopped
200 g/7 oz can tuna in brine
250 g/9 oz tub ricotta cheese

grated zest and juice
    of 1 lemon
1 tbsp freshly snipped chives
salt and freshly ground
    black pepper
8 dried cannelloni tubes
1 medium egg, beaten
125 g/4 oz cottage cheese

150 ml/¼ pint natural yogurt
pinch freshly grated nutmeg
50 g/2 oz mozzarella
    cheese, grated
tossed green salad, to serve

Preheat the oven to 190°C/375°F/Gas Mark 5, 10 minutes before cooking. Heat the olive oil in a frying pan and cook the spring onions and pepper until soft. Remove from the pan with a slotted draining spoon and place in a large bowl.

Drain the tuna, then stir into the spring onions and pepper. Beat the ricotta cheese with the grated lemon zest and juice, the snipped chives and salt and pepper to taste, until soft and blended. Add to the tuna and mix together. If the mixture is still a little stiff, add a little extra lemon juice.

With a teaspoon, carefully spoon the mixture into the cannelloni tubes, then lay the filled tubes in two medium lightly oiled shallow ovenproof dishes. Beat the egg, cottage cheese, natural yogurt and nutmeg together and pour over the cannelloni. Sprinkle with the grated mozzarella cheese and bake one of the dishes in the preheated oven for 15–20 minutes, or until the topping is golden brown and bubbling. Serve immediately with a tossed green salad.

Lightly cover the remaining dish and keep overnight in the refrigerator, or freeze if preferred.

HELPFUL HINT

This will keep for up to 1 month in the freezer. Thaw overnight in the refrigerator. Remember to switch the freezer to rapid freeze at least 2 hours before you put any food in to be frozen.

Saucy Cod & Pasta Bake

SERVES 2 + 1 DISH FOR FREEZING

450 g/1 lb fresh cod fillets,
  skinned
2 tbsp sunflower oil
1 onion, peeled and chopped
4 rashers streaky smoked
  bacon, rind removed,
  and chopped
150 g/5 oz baby button
  mushrooms, wiped

2 celery stalks, trimmed
  and thinly sliced
2 small courgettes, halved
  lengthways and sliced
400 g/7 oz can chopped
  tomatoes
100 ml/3 ½ fl oz fish stock
  or dry white wine
1 tbsp freshly chopped

tarragon
salt and freshly ground
  black pepper

For the pasta topping:
225–275 g/8–10 oz pasta shells
25 g/1 oz butter
4 tbsp plain flour
450 ml/¾ pint milk

Preheat the oven to 200°C/400°F/Gas Mark 6, 15 minutes before cooking. Cut the cod into bite-sized pieces and reserve.

Heat the sunflower oil in a large saucepan, add the onion and bacon and cook for 7–8 minutes. Add the mushrooms and celery and cook for 5 minutes, or until fairly soft. Add the courgettes and tomatoes to the bacon mixture and pour in the fish stock or wine. Bring to the boil, then simmer uncovered for 5 minutes, or until the sauce has thickened slightly. Remove from the heat and stir in the cod pieces and the tarragon. Season to taste with salt and pepper, then spoon into two lightly oiled medium-sized ovenproof dishes.

Meanwhile, bring a large pan of lightly salted water to a rolling boil. Add the pasta shells and cook according to the packet instructions, or until *al dente*.

For the topping, place the butter and flour in a saucepan and pour in the milk. Bring to the boil slowly, whisking until thickened and smooth. Drain the pasta thoroughly and stir into the sauce. Spoon carefully over both dishes with the fish mixture. Place in the preheated oven and bake for 20–25 minutes, or until the top is lightly browned and bubbling. Wrap, label and freeze the remaining dish. Use within 3–4 weeks.

HELPFUL HINT

Remember, when preparing food for the freezer it is important that none of it has been frozen before. If the food has been frozen before, it **must** be cooked thoroughly first, then it can be refrozen.

Traditional Lasagne

SERVES 2 + 1 DISH FOR FREEZING

1 tbsp olive oil
450 g/1 lb fresh lean minced beef steak
175 g/6 oz pancetta or smoked streaky bacon, chopped
1 large onion, peeled and chopped
2 celery stalks, trimmed and chopped
125 g/4 oz button mushrooms, wiped

and chopped
2 garlic cloves, peeled and chopped
100 g/3½ oz plain flour
300 ml/½ pint beef stock
1 tbsp freeze-dried mixed herbs
5 tbsp tomato purée
salt and freshly ground black pepper
75 g/3 oz butter
1 tsp English mustard powder

pinch freshly grated nutmeg
900 ml/1½ pints milk
125 g/4 oz Parmesan cheese, grated
125 g/4 oz Cheddar cheese, grated
8–12 precooked lasagne sheets

To serve:
crusty bread
fresh green salad leaves

Preheat the oven to 200°C/400°F/Gas Mark 6, 15 minutes before cooking. Heat the oil in a frying pan and cook the beef and pancetta in a large saucepan for 10 minutes, stirring to break up any lumps. Add the onion, celery and mushrooms and cook for 4 minutes, or until softened slightly. Stir in the garlic and 1 tablespoon of the flour and cook for 1 minute. Stir in the stock, herbs and tomato purée. Season to taste with salt and pepper. Bring to the boil, then cover, reduce the heat and simmer for 45 minutes.

Meanwhile, melt the butter in a small saucepan and stir in the remaining flour, mustard powder and nutmeg until well blended. Cook for 2 minutes. Remove from the heat and gradually blend in the milk until smooth. Return to the heat and bring to the boil, stirring, until thickened. Gradually stir in half of each cheese until melted. Season to taste. Spoon half the meat mixture into the base of two 600 ml/1 pint ovenproof dishes. Top with a single layer of pasta. Spread over half the sauce and scatter with half the cheese. Repeat layers, finishing with cheese. Bake in the oven for 30 minutes, or until the pasta is cooked and the top is golden brown and bubbling. Serve one lasagne immediately with crusty bread and a green salad. Freeze the other.

HELPFUL HINT

When using your freezer for storage, it is important that each dish is clearly labelled and dated, otherwise you might end up pulling out a dessert rather than a savoury dish for supper.

Cannelloni

**SERVES 2 + 1 DISH
FOR FREEZING**

2 tbsp olive oil
175 g/6 oz fresh pork mince
75 g/3 oz chicken livers,
    chopped
1 small onion, peeled
    and chopped
1 garlic clove, peeled
    and chopped
175 g/6 oz frozen chopped

spinach, thawed
1 tbsp freeze-dried oregano
pinch freshly grated nutmeg
salt and freshly ground
    black pepper
175 g/6 oz ricotta cheese
25 g/1 oz butter
25 g/1 oz plain flour
600 ml/1 pint milk

600 ml/1 pint ready-made
    tomato sauce
16 precooked cannelloni
    tubes
50 g/2 oz Parmesan
    cheese, grated
green salad, to serve

Preheat the oven to 190°C/375°F/Gas Mark 5, 10 minutes before cooking. Heat the olive oil in a frying pan and cook the mince and chicken livers for about 5 minutes, stirring occasionally, until browned all over. Break up any lumps, if necessary, with a wooden spoon.

Add the onion and garlic and cook for 4 minutes until softened. Add the spinach, oregano and nutmeg and season to taste with salt and pepper. Cook until all the liquid has evaporated, then remove the pan from the heat and allow to cool. Stir in the ricotta cheese.

Meanwhile, melt the butter in a small saucepan and stir in the plain flour to form a roux. Cook for 2 minutes, stirring occasionally. Remove from the heat and blend in the milk until smooth. Return to the heat and bring to the boil, stirring until the sauce has thickened. Reserve.

Spoon a thin layer of the tomato sauce on the bases of two 600 ml/1 pint ovenproof dishes. Divide the pork filling between the cannelloni tubes. Arrange on top of the tomato sauce. Spoon over the remaining tomato sauce. Pour over the white sauce and sprinkle with the Parmesan cheese. Bake one of the dishes in the preheated oven for 30–35 minutes, or until the cannelloni is tender and the top is golden brown. Serve immediately with a green salad. Freeze the other dish.

HELPFUL HINT

Allow the second dish to cool before freezing, then wrap and label. (By placing meals in polythene freezer bags as well you will ensure that they keep as moist as possible.)

Sausage & Redcurrant Pasta Bake

SERVES 2 + 1 DISH FOR FREEZING

450 g/1 lb good-quality thick pork sausages
2 tsp sunflower oil
25 g/1 oz butter
1 onion, peeled and sliced
2 tbsp plain white flour
450 ml/¾ pint chicken stock

150 ml/¼ pint port or good-quality red wine
1 tbsp freshly chopped thyme leaves, plus sprigs to garnish
1 bay leaf
4 tbsp redcurrant jelly

salt and freshly ground black pepper
350 g/12 oz fresh penne
75 g/3 oz Gruyère cheese, grated

Preheat the oven to 220°C/425°F/Gas Mark 7, 15 minutes before cooking. Prick the sausages, place in a shallow ovenproof dish and toss in the sunflower oil. Cook in the oven for 25–30 minutes, or until golden brown.

Meanwhile, melt the butter in a frying pan, add the onion and fry for 5 minutes, or until golden-brown. Stir in the flour and cook for 2 minutes. Remove the pan from the heat and gradually stir in the stock with the port or red wine. Return the pan to the heat and bring to the boil, stirring continuously until the sauce starts to thicken. Add the thyme, bay leaf and redcurrant jelly and season well with salt and pepper. Simmer the sauce for 5 minutes.

Bring a large pan of salted water to a rolling boil, add the pasta and cook for about 4 minutes, or until *al dente*. Drain thoroughly and reserve.

Lower the oven temperature to 200°C/400°F/Gas Mark 6. Remove the sausages from the oven and drain off any excess fat. Divide the sausages between two 600 ml/1 pint ovenproof dishes. Add the pasta. Pour over the sauce, removing the bay leaf, and toss together. Sprinkle with the Gruyère cheese and return to the oven for 15–20 minutes, or until bubbling and golden brown. Serve immediately, garnished with thyme sprigs. Freeze the remaining dish after cooking as before. Use within 2 weeks of freezing.

HELPFUL HINT
It is important to keep a list and to rotate the food in your freezer. This will ensure that none of your delicious meals are forgotten.

Gnocchi & Parma Ham Bake

**SERVES 2 + 1 DISH
FOR FREEZING**

3 tbsp olive oil
1 red onion, peeled and sliced
2 garlic cloves, peeled
175 g/6 oz plum tomatoes,
 skinned and quartered
2 tbsp sun-dried tomato purée
250 g/9 oz tub mascarpone

cheese
salt and freshly ground
 black pepper
1 tbsp freshly chopped
 tarragon
300 g/10 oz fresh gnocchi
125 g/4 oz Cheddar or

Parmesan cheese, grated
50 g/2 oz fresh white
 breadcrumbs
50 g/2 oz Parma ham, sliced
10 pitted green olives, halved
flat-leaf parsley sprigs,
 to garnish

Heat the oven to 180°C/350°F/Gas Mark 4, 10 minutes before cooking. Heat 2 tablespoons of the olive oil in a large frying pan and cook the onion and garlic for 5 minutes, or until softened. Stir in the tomatoes, sun-dried tomato purée and mascarpone cheese. Season to taste with salt and pepper. Add half the tarragon. Bring to the boil, then lower the heat immediately and simmer for 5 minutes.

Meanwhile, bring 1.7 litres/3 pints water to the boil in a large pan. Add the remaining olive oil and a good pinch of salt. Add the gnocchi and cook for 1–2 minutes, or until they rise to the surface.

Drain the gnocchi thoroughly and transfer to two medium-sized ovenproof dishes. Add the tomato sauce and toss gently to coat the gnocchi. Combine the Cheddar or Parmesan cheese with the breadcrumbs and remaining tarragon and scatter over the gnocchi mixture. Top with the Parma ham and olives and season again. Wrap, label and freeze one of the dishes. Use within two weeks of freezing. Cook the remaining dish in the preheated oven for 20–25 minutes, or until golden and bubbling. Serve immediately, garnished with parsley sprigs.

HELPFUL HINT

When thawing dishes, it is always advisable to do this in the refrigerator overnight.

Creamy Chicken Cannelloni

**SERVES 2 + 1 DISH
FOR FREEZING**

40 g/1½ oz butter
2 garlic cloves, peeled
and crushed
175 g/6 oz button
mushrooms, thinly sliced
1 tbsp freshly chopped basil
350 g/12 oz fresh spinach,
blanched
salt and freshly ground

black pepper
1½ tbsp plain flour
250 ml/8 fl oz chicken stock
150 ml/¼ pint dry white wine
85 ml/3 fl oz double cream
350 g/12 oz skinless,
boneless cooked chicken,
chopped
125 g/4 oz Parma ham,

finely chopped
½ tsp dried thyme
150 g/5 oz precooked
cannelloni tubes
125 g/4 oz Gruyère
cheese, grated
40 g/1½ oz Parmesan
cheese, grated
fresh basil sprig, to garnish

TASTY TIP

Whisk together 1 teaspoon
Dijon mustard, 2 teaspoons
lemon juice, a pinch sugar,
salt and pepper to taste and
2–3 tablespoons good-quality
olive oil. Use to coat 75 g/
3 oz mixed salad leaves.

Preheat the oven to 190°C/375°F/Gas Mark 5, 10 minutes before cooking. Lightly butter two medium-sized (750 ml/1¼ pint) ovenproof dishes. Heat half the butter in a large heavy-based frying pan, then add the garlic and mushrooms and cook gently for 5 minutes. Stir in the basil and spinach and cook, covered, until the spinach is wilted and just tender, stirring frequently. Season to taste with salt and pepper, then spoon into the dishes and reserve.

Melt the remaining butter in a small saucepan, then stir in the flour and cook for about 2 minutes, stirring constantly. Remove from the heat, stir in the stock, wine and cream. Return to the heat, bring to the boil and simmer until the sauce is thick and smooth, then season to taste. Measure 85 ml/3 fl oz of the cream sauce into a bowl. Add the chicken, Parma ham and dried thyme. Season to taste, then spoon the chicken mixture into the cannelloni tubes, arranging in two rows on top of the spinach layers.

Add half the Gruyère to the cream sauce and heat, stirring, until the cheese melts. Pour over the sauce and top with the remaining Gruyère and the Parmesan. Bake in the preheated oven for 35 minutes, or until golden and bubbling. Garnish with a sprig of fresh basil and serve immediately. Either freeze the remaining dish and use within 2–3 weeks, or keep in the refrigerator and use the next day.

Turkey & Mixed Mushroom Lasagne

SERVES 2 + 1 DISH FOR FREEZING

1 tbsp olive oil
225 g/8 oz mixed
   mushrooms e.g. button,
   chestnut and portabello,
   wiped and sliced
15 g/½ oz butter
25 g/1 oz plain flour
300 ml/½ pint skimmed milk
1 bay leaf

225 g/8 oz cooked turkey,
   cubed
¼ tsp freshly grated nutmeg
salt and freshly ground
   black pepper
400 g/14 oz can plum
   tomatoes, drained
   and chopped
1 tsp dried mixed herbs

9 lasagne sheets
   (about 150 g/5 oz)

For the topping:
200 ml/7 fl oz Greek yogurt
1 medium egg, lightly beaten
1 tbsp finely grated
   Parmesan cheese
mixed salad leaves, to serve

Preheat the oven to 180°C/350°F/Gas 4. Heat the oil and cook the mushrooms until tender and all the juices have evaporated. Remove and reserve.

Put the butter, flour, milk and bay leaf in the pan. Slowly bring to the boil, stirring until thickened. Simmer for 2–3 minutes. Remove the bay leaf and stir in the mushrooms, turkey, nutmeg, salt and pepper.

Mix together the tomatoes and mixed herbs and season with salt and pepper. Spoon half into the base of two 750 ml/1¼ pint ovenproof dishes. Top with 2 sheets of lasagne, breaking the lasagne sheets to fit the dish if necessary. Top with half the turkey mixture. Repeat the layers, then arrange the remaining pasta sheets on top.

Mix together the yogurt and egg. Spoon over the lasagne, spreading the mixture into the corners. Sprinkle with the Parmesan and bake in the preheated oven for 45 minutes. Serve one of the cooked lasagnes with the mixed salad.

HELPFUL HINT

Wrap, label and date the other cooked dish, freeze and use within 1 month. Remember to thaw in the refrigerator.

Courgette Lasagne

**SERVES 2 + 1 DISH
FOR FREEZING**

1 tbsp olive oil
1 small onion, peeled and
	finely chopped
125 g/4 oz mushrooms,
	wiped and thinly sliced
1–2 courgettes, trimmed and
	thinly sliced
2 garlic cloves, peeled and

finely chopped
½ tsp dried thyme
1 tbsp freshly chopped basil
	or flat-leaf parsley
salt and freshly ground
	black pepper
450 ml/¾ pint prepared white
	sauce (*see* page 250)

175 g/6 oz lasagne sheets,
	cooked
125 g/4 oz mozzarella
	cheese, grated
25 g/1 oz Parmesan
	cheese, grated
200g/7 oz canned chopped
	tomatoes, drained

Preheat the oven to 200°C/400°F/Gas Mark 6, 15 minutes before cooking. Heat the oil in a large frying pan, add the onion and cook for 3–5 minutes. Add the mushrooms, cook for 2 minutes then add the courgettes and cook for a further 3–4 minutes, or until tender. Stir in the garlic, thyme and basil or parsley and season to taste with salt and pepper. Remove from the heat and reserve.

Spoon one third of the white sauce on to the base of two 600 ml/1 pint lightly oiled ovenproof dishes. Arrange a layer of lasagne over the sauce, breaking the sheets to fit. Spread half the courgette mixture over the pasta, then sprinkle with some of the mozzarella and some of the Parmesan cheese. Repeat with more white sauce and another layer of lasagne, then cover with half the drained tomatoes.

Cover the tomatoes with lasagne, the remaining courgette mixture and some mozzarella and Parmesan cheese. Repeat the layers ending with a layer of lasagne sheets, white sauce and the remaining Parmesan cheese. Bake one of the dishes in the preheated oven for 35 minutes, or until golden. Serve immediately. Wrap and freeze the other dish and keep for up to 1 month.

**SERVES 2 + 1 DISH
FOR FREEZING**

Baked Macaroni Cheese

225 g/8 oz macaroni
40 g/1½ oz butter
1 onion, peeled and
   finely chopped
2 small leeks, trimmed,
   finely chopped
25 g/1 oz plain flour

350 ml/12 fl oz milk
1–2 dried bay leaves
½ tsp dried thyme
salt and freshly
   ground black pepper
cayenne pepper
freshly grated nutmeg

1 tbsp Dijon mustard
175 g/6 oz mature
   Cheddar cheese, grated
2 tbsp dried breadcrumbs
2 tbsp freshly grated
   Parmesan cheese
basil sprig, to garnish

Preheat the oven to 190˚C/375˚F/Gas Mark 5, 10 minutes before cooking. Bring a large pan of lightly salted water to a rolling boil. Add the macaroni and cook according to the packet instructions, or until *al dente*. Drain thoroughly and reserve.

Meanwhile, melt 40 g/1½ oz of the butter in a large heavy-based saucepan, add the onion and chopped leeks then cook, stirring frequently, for 5–7 minutes, or until softened. Sprinkle in the flour and cook, stirring constantly, for 2 minutes. Remove the pan from the heat, stir in the milk, return to the heat and cook, stirring, until a smooth sauce has formed.

Add the bay leaf and thyme to the sauce and season to taste with salt, pepper, cayenne pepper and freshly grated nutmeg. Simmer for about 15 minutes, stirring frequently, until thickened and smooth.

Remove the sauce from the heat. Add the mustard and Cheddar cheese and stir until the cheese has melted. Stir in the macaroni then tip into two lightly oiled 750 ml/1¼ pint ovenproof dishes.

Sprinkle the breadcrumbs and Parmesan cheese over the macaroni. Dot with the remaining butter, then bake one of the dishes in the preheated oven for 35–40 minutes or until golden. Garnish with a basil sprig and serve immediately.

HELPFUL HINT

If liked, the other dish will keep in the refrigerator for up to 3 days. Allow to cool then cover with kitchen foil or clingfilm. Remove before cooking.

Lamb & Potato Moussaka

700 g/1½ lb cooked
   roast lamb
700 g/1½ lb potatoes, peeled
125 g/4 oz butter
1 large onion, peeled
   and chopped
2–4 garlic cloves, peeled
and crushed
3 tbsp tomato purée
1 tbsp freshly chopped
   parsley
salt and freshly ground
   black pepper
3–4 tbsp olive oil
2 medium aubergines,
   trimmed and sliced
4 medium tomatoes, sliced
2 medium eggs
300 ml/½ pint Greek yogurt
2–3 tbsp Parmesan
   cheese, grated

Preheat the oven to 200˚C/400˚F/Gas Mark 6, about 15 minutes before required. Trim the lamb, discarding any fat then cut into fine dice and reserve. Thinly slice the potatoes and rinse thoroughly in cold water, then pat dry with a clean tea towel.

Melt 50 g/2 oz of the butter in a frying pan and fry the potatoes, in batches, until crisp and golden. Using a slotted spoon, remove from the pan and reserve. Use a third of the potatoes to line the base of two 750 ml/1¼ pint ovenproof dishes

Add the onion and garlic to the butter remaining in the pan and cook for 5 minutes. Add the lamb and fry for 1 minute. Blend the tomato purée with 3 tablespoons water and stir into the pan with the parsley and salt and pepper. Spoon over the layer of potatoes, then top with the remaining potato slices.

Heat the oil and the remaining butter in the pan and brown the aubergine slices for 5–6 minutes. Arrange the tomatoes on top of the potatoes, then the aubergines on top of the tomatoes. Beat the eggs with the yogurt and Parmesan cheese and pour over the aubergines and tomatoes. Wrap one of the dishes in freezer wrap, label and date then place in the freezer. Place the other dish on a baking sheet and cook in the preheated oven for 25 minutes, or until golden and piping hot. Serve.

HELPFUL HINT

The frozen moussaka will keep in the freezer for up to 2 months. When ready to use, allow to thaw overnight in the refrigerator, then cook as instructed.

Smoked Salmon Quiche

MAKES 2 QUICHES; EACH SERVING 2–4 SLICES

225 g/8 oz plain flour
50 g/2 oz butter
50 g/2 oz white vegetable
fat or lard
2 tsp sunflower oil
225 g/8 oz potato, peeled
and diced

125 g/4 oz Gruyère
cheese, grated
75 g/3 oz smoked salmon
trimmings
5 medium eggs, beaten
300 ml/½ pint single cream
salt and freshly ground

black pepper
1 tbsp freshly chopped
flat-leaf parsley

To serve:
mixed salad
baby new potatoes

Preheat the oven to 200°C/400°F/Gas Mark 6. Blend the flour, butter and white vegetable fat or lard together until it resembles fine breadcrumbs. Blend again, adding sufficient water to make a firm but pliable dough. Use the dough to line two 15 cm/6 inch loose-bottomed flan tins, then chill the pastry cases in the refrigerator for 30 minutes. Bake blind with baking beans for 10 minutes.

Heat the oil in a small frying pan, add the diced potato and cook for 3–4 minutes until lightly browned. Reduce the heat and cook for 2–3 minutes, or until tender. Leave to cool.

Scatter the grated cheese evenly over the base of the pastry cases, then arrange the cooled potato on top. Add the smoked salmon in an even layer.

Beat the eggs with the cream and season to taste with salt and pepper. Whisk in the parsley and pour the mixture carefully over the salmon mixture in both cases. Place on two separate baking sheets.

Reduce the oven to 180°C/350°F/Gas Mark 4 and bake for about 30–40 minutes, or until the filling is set and golden. Serve hot or cold with a mixed salad and baby new potatoes.

HELPFUL HINT

Wrap and label one of the quiches, freeze and keep for up to 1 month. When ready to use, warm for 10–15 minutes in a moderately hot oven for 15 minutes.

Smoked Haddock Tart

SERVES 2–4

For the shortcrust pastry:
150 g/5 oz plain flour
pinch salt
25 g/1 oz white vegetable
    fat, cut into small cubes
40 g/1½ oz butter or hard
    margarine, cut into
    small cubes

For the filling:
225 g/8 oz smoked haddock,
    skinned and cubed
2 large eggs, beaten
300 ml/½ pint double cream
1 tsp Dijon mustard
freshly ground black pepper
125 g/4 oz Gruyère

cheese, grated
1 tbsp freshly
    snipped chives

To serve:
lemon wedges
tomato wedges
fresh green salad leaves

Preheat the oven to 190°C/375°F/Gas Mark 5. Sift the flour and salt into a large bowl. Add the fats and mix lightly. Using the fingertips rub into the flour until the mixture resembles breadcrumbs.

Sprinkle 1 tablespoon cold water into the mixture and, with a knife, start bringing the dough together. (It may be necessary to use the hands for the final stage.) If the dough does not form a ball instantly, add a little more water. Put the pastry in a polythene bag and chill for at least 30 minutes.

On a lightly floured surface, roll out the pastry and use to line a 18 cm/7 inch lightly oiled quiche or flan tin. Prick the base all over with a fork and bake blind in the preheated oven for 15 minutes. Carefully remove the pastry from the oven, brush with a little of the beaten egg. Return to the oven for a further 5 minutes, then place the fish in the pastry case.

For the filling, beat together the eggs and cream. Add the mustard, black pepper and cheese and pour over the fish. Sprinkle with the chives and bake for 35–40 minutes or until the filling is golden brown and set in the centre. Serve hot or cold with the lemon and tomato wedges and salad leaves.

HELPFUL HINT

Cover any remaining tart lightly, once cold, with clingfilm or kitchen foil and leave in the refrigerator. Use within 2 days of making.

Luxury Fish Pasties

**SERVES 2 + 4
FOR FREEZING**

2 quantities of quick flaky
    pastry (*see* page 299),
    chilled
125 g/4 oz butter
125 g/4 oz plain flour
300 ml/½ pint milk
225 g/8 oz salmon fillet,

skinned and cut
    into chunks
1 tbsp freshly chopped
    parsley
1 tbsp freshly chopped dill
grated zest and juice of 1 lime
225 g/8 oz peeled prawns

salt and freshly ground
    black pepper
1 small egg, beaten
1 tsp sea salt (optional)
fresh green salad leaves,
    to serve

Preheat the oven to 200°C/400°F/Gas Mark 6. Place the butter in a saucepan and slowly heat until melted.

Add the flour and cook, stirring for 1 minute. Remove from the heat and gradually add the milk a little at a time, stirring between each addition.

Return to the heat and simmer, stirring continuously until thickened. Remove from the heat and add the salmon, parsley, dill, lime zest, lime juice, prawns and seasoning.

Roll out the pastry on a lightly floured surface and cut out six 12.5 cm/5 inch circles and six 10 cm/4 inch circles. Brush the edges of the smaller circle with the beaten egg and place two tablespoons of filling in the centre of each one. Place the larger circle over the filling and press the edges together to seal.

Pinch the edge of the pastry between the forefinger and thumb to ensure a firm seal and decorative edge. Cut a slit in each parcel, brush with the beaten egg and sprinkle with sea salt, if using. Transfer to a baking sheet and cook in the preheated oven for 20 minutes, or until golden brown. Serve immediately with some fresh green salad leaves and freeze the remaining four pasties once cooled.

HELPFUL HINT

If none of the ingredients have been frozen before, the pasties can be frozen uncooked. Open freeze, then wrap, label and date. Keep for up to 1 month and thaw in the refrigerator overnight.

Panzerotti

**MAKES 4 TO EAT NOW
+ 4 FOR FREEZING**

225 g/8 oz strong white flour
pinch salt
½ tsp easy-blend dried yeast
1 tbsp olive oil
150 ml/¼ pint warm water
fresh rocket leaves, to serve

For the filling:
2 tsp olive oil

1 tbsp finely chopped
  red onion,
1 garlic clove, peeled
  and crushed
1 tbsp yellow pepper,
  deseeded and chopped
1 small courgette, about
  40 g g/1½ oz, trimmed
  and chopped

25 g/1 oz black olives, pitted
  and quartered
50 g/2 oz mozzarella cheese,
  cut into tiny cubes
salt and freshly ground
  black pepper
2–3 tbsp tomato purée
1 tsp dried mixed herbs
oil for deep-frying

Sift the flour and salt into a bowl. Stir in the yeast. Make a well in the centre. Add the oil and the warm water and mix to a soft dough. Knead on a lightly floured surface until smooth and elastic. Put in an oiled bowl, cover and leave in a warm place to rise while making the filling.

To make the filling, heat the oil in a frying pan and cook the onion for 5 minutes. Add the garlic, pepper and courgette. Cook for 5 minutes, or until the vegetables are tender. Tip into a bowl and leave to cool slightly. Stir in the olives, mozzarella and season to taste with salt and pepper.

Briefly knead the dough. Divide into 8 equal pieces. Roll out each to a circle about 10 cm/ 4 inches in diameter. Mix together the tomato purée and dried herbs, then spread about 1 teaspoon on each circle, leaving a 2 cm/¾ inch border around the edge. Divide the filling equally between the circles. It will seem a small amount, but if you overfill, they will leak during cooking. Brush the edges with water, then fold in half to enclose the filling. Press to seal, then crimp the edges.

Heat the oil in a deep-fat fryer to 180°C/350°F. Deep-fry the panzerotti in batches for 3 minutes, or until golden. Drain on absorbent kitchen paper and keep warm in a low oven until ready to serve with fresh rocket.

HELPFUL HINT
Leave the panzerotti you wish to freeze until cold, then wrap, label, date and freeze. Keep for up to 1 month. Thaw in the refrigerator and reheat gently in a moderately hot oven.

Bacon, Mushroom & Cheese Puffs

1 tbsp olive oil
225 g/8 oz field mushrooms, wiped and roughly chopped
225 g/8 oz streaky bacon, rind removed, and roughly chopped

2 tbsp freshly chopped parsley
salt and freshly ground black pepper
350 g/12 oz ready-rolled puff pastry sheet, thawed if frozen

25 g/1 oz Emmenthal cheese, grated
1 medium egg, beaten
salad leaves such as rocket or watercress, to garnish
tomatoes, to serve

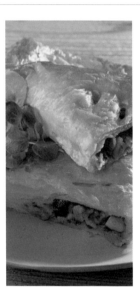

Preheat the oven to 200˚C/400˚F/Gas Mark 6. Heat the olive oil in a large frying pan. Add the mushrooms and bacon and fry for 6–8 minutes until golden in colour. Stir in the parsley, season to taste with salt and pepper and allow to cool.

Roll the sheet of pastry a little thinner on a lightly floured surface to a 30.5 cm/12 inch square. Cut the pastry into 4 equal squares.

Stir the grated Emmenthal cheese into the mushroom mixture. Spoon a quarter of the mixture on to one half of each square. Brush the edges of the squares with a little of the beaten egg.

Fold over the pastry to form a triangular parcel. Seal the edges well and place on a lightly oiled baking sheet. Repeat until the squares are done. Make shallow slashes in the top of each parcel with a knife.

Brush the parcels with the remaining beaten egg and cook in the preheated oven for 20 minutes, or until puffy and golden brown.

Serve warm or cold, garnished with the salad leaves and served with tomatoes.

HELPFUL HINT

The cooked puffs will keep, if lightly covered with kitchen foil or clingfilm, in the refrigerator for up to 3 days. Or, wrap, label and freeze for up to 1 month. They are best eaten if warmed through first.

Cheese & Onion Oat Pie

SERVES 2 +
4 PORTIONS FOR LATER

1 tbsp sunflower oil,
plus 1 tsp
25 g/1 oz butter
2 medium onions,
peeled and sliced
1 garlic clove, peeled

and crushed
150 g/5 oz porridge oats
125 g/4 oz mature Cheddar
cheese, grated
2 medium eggs,
lightly beaten

2 tbsp freshly chopped
parsley
salt and freshly ground
black pepper
300 g/10 oz baking
potato, peeled

Preheat the oven to 180°C/350°F/Gas Mark 4. Heat the oil and half the butter in a saucepan until melted. Add the onions and garlic and gently cook for 10 minutes, or until soft. Remove from the heat and tip into a large bowl.

Spread the oats out on a baking sheet and toast in the hot oven for 12 minutes. Leave to cool, then add to the onions with the cheese, eggs and parsley. Season to taste with salt and pepper and mix well.

Line the base of a 20.5 cm/8 inch round sandwich tin with greaseproof paper and oil well. Thinly slice the potato and arrange the slices on the base, overlapping them slightly.

Spoon the cheese and oat mixture on top of the potato, spreading evenly with the back of a spoon. Cover with kitchen foil and bake for 30 minutes.

HELPFUL HINT

Any remaining pie will keep for up to 2 days if lightly wrapped and stored in the refrigerator. This would make an excellent lunchbox addition.

Invert the pie onto a baking sheet so that the potatoes are on top. Carefully remove the tin and lining paper.

Preheat the grill to medium. Melt the remaining butter and carefully brush over the potato topping. Cook under the preheated grill for 5–6 minutes until the potatoes are lightly browned. Cut into wedges and serve.

Potato &
Goats' Cheese Tart

SERVES 2 +
4 PORTIONS FOR LATER

275 g/10 oz prepared
   shortcrust pastry,
   thawed if frozen
550 g/1¼ lb small waxy
   potatoes
salt and freshly ground
   black pepper

beaten egg, for brushing
2 tbsp sun-dried
   tomato purée
¼ tsp chilli powder, or to taste
1 large egg
150 ml/¼ pint sour cream
150 ml/¼ pint milk

2 tbsp freshly snipped chives
325 g/11 oz goats'
   cheese, sliced
salad and warm crusty
   bread, to serve

Preheat the oven to 190°C/375°F/Gas Mark 5, about 10 minutes before cooking. Roll the pastry out on a lightly floured surface and use to line a 23 cm/9 inch fluted flan tin. Chill in the refrigerator for 30 minutes.

Scrub the potatoes, place in a large saucepan of lightly salted water and bring to the boil. Simmer for 10–15 minutes, or until the potatoes are tender. Drain and reserve until cool enough to handle.

Line the pastry case with greaseproof paper and baking beans or crumpled kitchen foil and bake blind in the preheated oven for 15 minutes. Remove from the oven and discard the paper and beans or foil. Brush the base with a little beaten egg, then return to the oven and cook for a further 5 minutes. Remove from the oven.

HELPFUL HINT
This tart will keep for up to 2 days in the refrigerator. Keep lightly covered.

Cut the potatoes into 1 cm/½ inch thick slices; reserve. Spread the sun-dried tomato purée over the base of the pastry case, sprinkle with the chilli powder, then arrange the potato slices on top in a decorative pattern. Beat together the egg, sour cream, milk and chives, then season to taste with salt and pepper. Pour over the potatoes. Arrange the goats' cheese on top. Bake in the preheated oven for 30 minutes until golden brown and set. Serve immediately with salad and warm bread.

Stilton, Tomato & Courgette Quiche

**SERVES 2 + 2 PORTIONS
FOR LUNCH THE NEXT DAY**

1 quantity shortcrust
pastry (*see* page 264)
25 g/1 oz butter
1 onion, peeled and
finely chopped

1 courgette, trimmed
and sliced
125 g/4 oz Stilton cheese,
crumbled
6 cherry tomatoes, halved

2 large eggs, beaten
200 ml/7 fl oz tub
crème fraîche
salt and freshly ground
black pepper

Preheat the oven to 190°C/375°F/Gas Mark 5. On a lightly floured surface, roll out the pastry and use to line an 18 cm/7 inch lightly oiled quiche or flan tin, trimming any excess pastry with a knife.

Prick the base all over with a fork and bake blind in the preheated oven for 15 minutes. Remove the pastry from the oven and brush with a little of the beaten egg. Return to the oven for a further 5 minutes.

Heat the butter in a frying pan and gently fry the onion and courgette for about 4 minutes until soft and starting to brown. Transfer into the pastry case.

Sprinkle the Stilton over evenly and top with the halved cherry tomatoes.

Beat together the eggs and crème fraîche and season to taste with salt and pepper. Pour into the pastry case and bake in the oven for 35–40 minutes, or until the filling is golden brown and set in the centre. Serve the quiche hot and cold the next day.

HELPFUL HINT

This quiche is ideal to take
on a picnic or in a lunchbox.

French Onion Tart

**MAKES 2 TARTS:
1 FOR NOW & 1 FOR FREEZING**

For the quick flaky pastry:
125 g/4 oz butter
175 g/6 oz plain flour
pinch salt

For the filling:
2 tbsp olive oil
4 large onions, peeled
    and thinly sliced
3 tbsp white wine vinegar
2 tbsp muscovado sugar

a little beaten egg or milk
175 g/6 oz Cheddar
    cheese, grated
salt and freshly ground
    black pepper

Preheat the oven to 200°C/400°F/Gas Mark 6. Place the butter in the freezer for 30 minutes. Sift the flour and salt into a large bowl. Remove the butter from the freezer and grate using the coarse side of a grater, dipping the butter in the flour every now and again as it makes it easier to grate. Mix the butter into the flour, using a knife, making sure all the butter is coated thoroughly with flour. Add 2 tablespoons cold water and continue to mix, bringing the mixture together. Use your hands to complete the mixing. Add a little more water if needed to leave a clean bowl. Place the pastry in a polythene bag and chill in the refrigerator for 30 minutes.

Heat the oil in a large frying pan, then fry the onions for 10 minutes, stirring occasionally until softened. Stir in the white wine vinegar and sugar. Increase the heat and stir frequently, for another 4–5 minutes until the onions turn a deep caramel colour. Cook for another 5 minutes, then reserve to cool.

Cut the pastry in half and, on a lightly floured surface, roll out one half and cut out an 18 cm/ 7 inch circle. Wrap over a rolling pin and move the circle onto a baking sheet. Repeat with the other pastry half. Sprinkle 40 g/1½ oz of the cheese over each of the circles, leaving a 5 cm/ 2 inch border around the edge, then spoon the onions over the cheese. Fold the uncovered pastry edges over the edge of the filling to form a rim, and brush the rim with beaten egg or milk. Season to taste with salt and pepper. Sprinkle the remaining cheese over both pastry cases. Bake one of the tarts for 20–25 minutes. Transfer to a large plate and serve immediately.

HELPFUL HINT

The remaining tart can be frozen uncooked on a baking sheet. Once frozen, wrap in freezer wrap, label and date. It will keep in the freezer for up to 2 months. Thaw overnight in the refrigerator before cooking.

Garlic Wild Mushroom Galettes

**SERVES 2 +
2 FOR LATER**

1 quantity quick flaky pastry
(*see* page 273, chilled
1 onion, peeled
1 red chilli, deseeded
2 garlic cloves, peeled
300 g/10 oz mixed

mushrooms (e.g. oyster,
chestnut, morels, ceps
and chanterelles)
25 g/1 oz butter
2 tbsp freshly chopped
parsley

125 g/4 oz mozzarella
cheese, sliced

To serve:
cherry tomatoes
mixed green salad leaves

Preheat the oven to 220°C/425°F/Gas Mark 7. On a lightly floured surface roll out the chilled pastry very thinly. Cut out four 15 cm/6 inch circles and place on a lightly oiled baking sheet.

Slice the onion thinly, then divide into rings and reserve. Slice the chilli thinly and slice the garlic into wafer-thin slivers. Add to the onions and reserve.

Wipe or lightly rinse the mushrooms. Halve or quarter any large mushrooms and keep the small ones whole.

Heat the butter in a frying pan and fry the onion, chilli and garlic gently for about 3 minutes. Add the mushrooms and cook for about 5 minutes, or until beginning to soften. Stir the parsley into the mushroom mixture and drain off any excess liquid.

Pile the mushroom mixture onto the pastry circles within 5 mm/¼ inch of the edge. Arrange the sliced mozzarella cheese on top. Bake in the preheated oven for 12–15 minutes, or until golden brown and serve with the tomatoes and salad.

HELPFUL HINT

If liked, cook 2 galettes then place the remaining filling in a small bowl, and the pastry rounds on a clean baking tray, cover and store both overnight in the refrigerator. Cook the next evening.

Olive & Feta Parcels

MAKES 30

1 small red pepper	black olives	6 sheets filo pastry
1 small yellow pepper	125 g/4 oz feta cheese	3 tbsp olive oil
125 g/4 oz assorted	2 tbsp pine nuts,	sour cream and chive dip,
marinated green and	lightly toasted	to serve

Preheat the oven to 180°C/350°F/Gas Mark 4. Preheat the grill, then line the grill rack with kitchen foil.

Cut the peppers into quarters and remove the seeds. Place skin-side up on the foil-lined grill rack and cook under the preheated grill for 10 minutes, turning occasionally until the skins begin to blacken. Place the peppers in a polythene bag and leave until cool enough to handle, then skin and slice thinly.

Chop the olives and cut the feta cheese into small cubes. Mix together the olives, feta, sliced peppers and pine nuts.

Cut 1 sheet of filo pastry in half then brush with a little of the oil. Place a spoonful of the olive and feta mix about one third of the way up the pastry. Fold over the pastry and wrap to form a square parcel encasing the filling completely.

Place this parcel in the centre of the second half of the pastry sheet. Brush the edges lightly with a little oil, bring up the corners to meet in the centre and twist them loosely to form a purse.

Brush with a little more oil and repeat with the remaining filo pastry and filling. Place the parcels on a lightly oiled baking sheet and bake in the preheated oven for 10–15 minutes, or until crisp and golden brown. Serve with the dip.

HELPFUL HINT

Open freeze remaining parcels, then place in a freezeable container, label, date and freeze for up to 1 month. Thaw overnight in the refrigerator or cook from frozen, allowing an extra 8–10 minutes in the oven.

Soft Dinner Rolls

MAKES 16

50 g/2 oz butter
1 tbsp caster sugar
225 ml/8 fl oz milk
550 g/1¼ lb strong

white flour
1½ tsp salt
2 tsp easy-blend dried yeast
2 medium eggs, beaten

To glaze and finish:
2 tbsp milk
1 tsp sea salt
2 tsp poppy seeds

Preheat the oven to 220°C/425°F/Gas Mark 7–15 minutes before baking. Gently heat the butter, sugar and milk in a saucepan until the butter has melted and the sugar has dissolved. Cool until tepid.

Sift the flour and salt into a bowl, stir in the yeast and make a well in the centre. Reserve 1 tablespoon of the beaten eggs. Add the rest to the dry ingredients with the milk mixture. Mix to form a soft dough.

Knead the dough on a lightly floured surface for 10 minutes until smooth and elastic. Put in an oiled bowl, cover with clingfilm and leave in a warm place to rise for 1 hour, or until doubled in size. Knead again for a minute or two, then divide into 16 pieces. Shape into plaits, snails, clover leaves and cottage buns. Place on 2 oiled baking sheets, cover with oiled clingfilm and leave to rise for 30 minutes, until doubled in size.

Mix the reserved beaten egg with the milk and brush over the rolls. Sprinkle some with sea salt, others with poppy seeds and leave some plain. Bake in the preheated oven for about 20 minutes, or until golden and hollow sounding when tapped underneath. Transfer to a wire rack. Cover with a clean tea towel while cooling to keep the rolls soft, and serve.

HELPFUL HINT

Open freeze, then place in polythene freezer bags, label and date. When required, simply remove as many as required and allow to thaw at room temperature for 1–2 hours.

Rosemary & Olive Focaccia

MAKES 2 LOAVES

700 g/1½ lb strong
   white flour
pinch salt
pinch caster sugar
10 g/¼ oz sachet easy-blend
   dried yeast
2 tsp freshly chopped

rosemary
450 ml/¾ pint warm water
3 tbsp olive oil
75 g/3 oz pitted black olives,
   roughly chopped
rosemary sprigs,
   to garnish

To finish:
3 tbsp olive oil
coarse sea salt
freshly ground black pepper

Preheat the oven to 200°C/400°F/Gas Mark 6, 15 minutes before baking. Sift the flour, salt and sugar into a large bowl. Stir in the yeast and rosemary. Make a well in the centre. Pour in the warm water and the oil and mix to a soft dough. Turn out on to a lightly floured surface and knead for about 10 minutes, until smooth and elastic.

Pat the olives dry on kitchen paper, then gently knead into the dough. Put in an oiled bowl, cover with clingfilm and leave to rise in a warm place for 1½ hours, or until it has doubled in size.

Turn out the dough and knead again for a minute or two. Divide in half and roll out each piece to a 25.5 cm/10 inch circle. Transfer to oiled baking sheets, cover with oiled clingfilm and leave to rise for 30 minutes.

Using the fingertips, make deep dimples all over the dough. Drizzle with the oil and sprinkle with sea salt.

Bake in the preheated oven for 20–25 minutes, or until risen and golden. Cool on a wire rack and garnish with rosemary sprigs. Grind over a little black pepper before serving.

HELPFUL HINT

Try and use within 2–3 days of making. If this is not possible, open freeze once the bread is cold, then wrap and label. Use within 2 weeks of freezing and warm before eating.

Desserts & Cakes

Raspberry Soufflé

SERVES 2 + 2 FOR FREEZING

125 g/4 oz redcurrants
50 g/2 oz caster sugar
1 sachet (3 tsp)
   powdered gelatine

3 medium eggs, separated
300 g/½ pint Greek yogurt
450 g/1 lb fresh raspberries

To decorate:
mint sprigs
extra fruits

Wrap a band of double thickness greaseproof paper around four 150 ml/¼ pint ramekin dishes, making sure that 5 cm/2 inches of the paper stays above the top of each dish. Secure the paper to the dish with string, an elastic band or sticky tape.

Place the redcurrants and 1 tablespoon of the sugar in a small saucepan. Cook for 5 minutes until softened. Remove from the heat, sieve and reserve.

Place 3 tablespoons water in a small bowl and sprinkle over the gelatine. Allow to stand for 5 minutes until spongy. Place the bowl over a pan of simmering water and leave until dissolved. Remove and allow to cool.

Beat together the remaining sugar and egg yolks until pale thick and creamy, then fold in the yogurt with a metal spoon or rubber spatula until well blended.

HELPFUL HINT

The soufflés and redcurrant purée will keep for up to 1 month in the freezer. Allow to thaw overnight in the refrigerator. Decorate as instructed.

Sieve the raspberries and fold into the yogurt mixture with the gelatine. Whisk the egg whites until stiff and fold into the yogurt mixture. Pour into the prepared dishes and chill in the refrigerator for at least 2 hours, longer if time permits, until firm.

When ready to serve, remove the paper from the dishes and spread the redcurrant purée over the top of the soufflés. Decorate with mint sprigs and extra fruits and serve.

Frozen Amaretti Soufflé with Strawberries

2 + 2 FOR FREEZING

50 g/2 oz Amaretti biscuits
4–5 tbsp Amaretto liqueur
grated zest and juice of
    ½ lemon
2 tsp powdered gelatine

3 medium eggs, separated
75 g/3 oz soft brown sugar
300 ml/½ pint double cream
225 g/8 oz fresh strawberries,
    halved if large

1 tsp vanilla extract
1 tbsp caster sugar
few finely crushed Amaretti
    biscuits, to decorate

Set the freezer to rapid-freeze at least 2 hours before you need it. Wrap a collar of greaseproof paper around four 150 ml/¼ pint individual ramekin dishes to extend at least 5 cm/2 inches above the rim and secure with string. Break the Amaretti biscuits into a bowl. Sprinkle over 3 tablespoons of the Amaretto liqueur and leave to soak.

Put the lemon zest and juice into a small heatproof bowl and sprinkle over the gelatine. Leave for 5 minutes to sponge, then put the bowl over a saucepan of simmering water, ensuring that the base of the bowl does not touch the water. Stir occasionally until the gelatine has dissolved completely. In a clean bowl, whisk the egg yolks and sugar until thick and creamy and then stir in the gelatine and the soaked biscuits. In another bowl, lightly whip 250 ml/8 fl oz of the cream and, using a large metal spoon or rubber spatula, fold into the mixture. In a third clean bowl, whisk the egg whites until stiff, then fold into the soufflé mixture. Transfer to the prepared individual ramekin dishes, and level the top. Freeze for at least 8 hours, or preferably overnight. Remember to return the freezer to its normal setting when you have finished.

Put the strawberries into a bowl with the vanilla extract and sugar and remaining Amaretto liqueur. Leave overnight in the refrigerator, then allow to come to room temperature before serving.

When required, place the soufflés in the refrigerator for about 1 hour. Whip the remaining cream and use to decorate the soufflés, then sprinkle a few finely crushed Amaretti biscuits on the top and serve with the strawberries.

HELPFUL HINT

Leave the two remaining soufflés in the freezer for up to 1 month. Serve as above.

Crème Brûlée with Sugared Raspberries

300 ml/½ pint fresh
   whipping cream
2 medium egg yolks
40 g/1½ oz caster sugar

few drops vanilla extract
25 g/1 oz demerara sugar
75 g/3 oz fresh raspberries

Preheat the oven to 150°C/300°F/Gas Mark 2. Pour the cream into a bowl and place over a saucepan of gently simmering water. Heat gently but do not allow to boil.

Meanwhile, whisk together the egg yolks, 25 g/1 oz of the caster sugar and the vanilla extract. When the cream is warm, pour it over the egg mixture briskly whisking until it is mixed completely.

Pour into two individual ramekin dishes and place in a roasting tin. Fill the tin with sufficient water to come halfway up the sides of the dishes.

Bake in the preheated oven for about 1 hour, or until the puddings are set. (To test if set, carefully insert a round bladed knife into the centre, if the knife comes out clean they are set.) Remove the puddings from the roasting tin and allow to cool. Chill in the refrigerator, preferably overnight.

Sprinkle the demerara sugar over the top of each dish and place the puddings under a preheated hot grill. When the sugar has caramelised and turned deep brown, remove from the heat and cool. Chill the puddings in the refrigerator for 2–3 hours before serving.

Toss the raspberries in the remaining caster sugar and sprinkle over the top of each dish. Serve with a little extra cream if liked.

Grape & Almond Layer

SERVES 2

150 ml/¼ pint fromage frais
150 ml/¼ pint Greek-
    style yogurt
1–2 tbsp icing sugar, sifted

1 tbsp crème de cassis
225 g/8 oz red grapes
75 g/3 oz Amaretti biscuits
1 ripe passion fruit

To decorate:
icing sugar
extra grapes, optional

Mix together the fromage frais and yogurt in a bowl and lightly fold in the sifted icing sugar and crème de cassis with a large metal spoon or rubber spatula until lightly blended.

Using a small knife, remove the seeds from the grapes if necessary. Rinse lightly and pat dry on absorbent kitchen paper.

Place the deseeded grapes in a bowl and stir in any juice from the grapes from deseeding.

Place the Amaretti biscuits in a polythene bag and crush roughly with a rolling pin. (Alternatively, use a food processor.)

Cut the passion fruit in half, scoop out the seeds with a teaspoon and reserve.

Divide the yogurt mixture between two tall glasses, then layer alternately with grapes, crushed biscuits and most of the passion fruit seeds. Finish with a layer of the yogurt mixture and the remaining passion fruit seeds. Chill for 1 hour and decorate with extra grapes. Lightly dust with icing sugar and serve.

Maple Pears with Pistachios & Simple Chocolate Sauce

SERVES 2

15 g/½ oz unsalted butter
25 g/1 oz unsalted pistachios
2 medium-ripe firm pears,
   peeled, quartered
   and cored
1 tsp lemon juice

pinch ground
   ginger (optional)
3 tbsp maple syrup

For the chocolate sauce:
75 ml/3 fl oz double cream

1 tbsp milk
few drops vanilla extract
75 g/3 oz plain dark
   chocolate, broken
   into squares and
   roughly chopped

Melt the butter in a deep frying pan or wok over a medium heat until sizzling. Turn down the heat a little, add the pistachios and stir-fry for 30 seconds.

Add the pears to the pan and continue cooking for about 2–4 minutes, turning frequently and carefully, until the nuts are beginning to brown and the pears are tender.

Add the lemon juice, ground ginger, if using, and maple syrup. Cook for 3–4 minutes, or until the syrup has reduced slightly. Spoon the pears and the syrup into a serving dish and leave to cool for 1–2 minutes while making the chocolate sauce.

Pour the cream and milk into the pan. Add the vanilla extract and heat just to boiling point. Remove the wok from the heat.

Add the chocolate to the pan and leave for 1 minute to melt, then stir until the chocolate is evenly mixed with the cream. Pour into a jug and serve while still warm, with the pears.

Chocolate Fruit Tiramisu

SERVES 2

1 ripe passion fruit
1 fresh nectarine or peach
40 g/1½ oz sponge
    finger biscuits
50 g/2 oz Amaretti biscuits

2–3 tbsp Amaretti liqueur
3 tbsp prepared black coffee
125 g/4 oz mascarpone
    cheese
200 ml/7 fl oz fresh custard

75 g/3 oz plain dark
    chocolate, finely
    chopped or grated
1 tbsp cocoa powder,
    sifted

Cut the passion fruit in half, scoop out the seeds and reserve. Plunge the nectarine or peach into boiling water and leave for 2–3 minutes. Carefully remove the fruit from the water, cut in half and remove the stone. Peel off the skin, chop the flesh finely and reserve.

Break the sponge finger biscuits and Amaretti biscuits in half. Place the Amaretti liqueur and prepared black coffee into a shallow dish and stir well. Place half the sponge fingers and Amaretti biscuits into the Amaretti and coffee mixture and soak for 30 seconds. Lift out both biscuits from the liquor and arrange in the bases of two deep individual glass dishes.

Cream the mascarpone cheese until soft and creamy, then slowly beat in the fresh custard and mix well together. Spoon half the mascarpone mixture over the biscuits in the dishes and sprinkle with half the finely chopped or grated dark chocolate.

Arrange half the passion fruit seeds and the chopped fruit over the chocolate and sprinkle with half the sifted cocoa powder. Place the remaining biscuits in the remaining coffee liqueur mixture and soak for 30 seconds, then arrange on top of the fruit and cocoa powder. Top with the remaining chopped or grated chocolate, chopped fruit and the mascarpone cheese mixture, piling the mascarpone high in the dishes.

Chill in the refrigerator for 1½ hours, then spoon the remaining passion fruit seeds and cocoa powder over the desserts. Chill in the refrigerator for 30 minutes and serve.

Fruited French Toast

SERVES 2

4 slices spicy fruit loaf,
about 1 cm/½ inch thick
125 ml/4 fl oz milk
2 tbsp orange liqueur
1 medium egg yolk
¼ tsp, or to taste,
ground cinnamon
25 g/1 oz unsalted butter

1 tbsp sunflower oil
2–3 tbsp seedless raspberry
jam or conserve

For the orange-scented cream:
125 ml/4 fl oz whipping
cream
1 tsp icing sugar

1 tbsp finely grated
orange zest
2 tsp orange flower water
or orange juice

Cut the crusts off the bread, then cut each slice diagonally into 4 triangles. Mix together half the milk and 1 tablespoon of the liqueur. Quickly dip the bread triangles in the mixture, then place on a wire rack over a tray to drain.

Beat together the egg yolk, cinnamon, remaining milk and any liqueur-flavoured milk on the tray. Dip the triangles in the egg and return to the rack.

Heat half the butter and the oil in a frying pan or wok. Add the bread triangles about 3 at a time and fry on both sides until well browned. Remove and keep warm in a low oven, while cooking the rest. When needed, add the remaining butter and finish cooking the bread triangles. Add to those keeping warm in the oven while making the sauce.

Gently heat the jam in a small saucepan or wok with the remaining 1 tablespoon of liqueur and 1 tablespoon water until melted, then cook for 1 minute.

To make the orange-scented cream, whisk the cream, icing sugar, orange zest and orange flower water or juice together until soft peaks form. Serve the French toasts drizzled with the jam sauce and accompanied by the orange-scented cream.

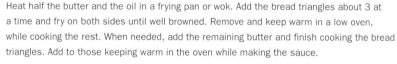

Stir–fried Banana & Peaches with Rum Butterscotch Sauce

SERVES 2

1 medium-firm banana
2 tsp caster sugar
2 tsp lime juice
2 firm, ripe peaches
   or nectarines

2 tsp sunflower oil

For the rum
   butterscotch sauce:
25 g/1 oz unsalted butter

25 g/1 oz soft light
   brown sugar
50 g/2 oz demerara sugar
150 ml/¼ pint double cream
1 tbsp dark rum

Peel the banana and cut into 2.5 cm/1 inch diagonal slices. Place in a bowl and sprinkle with the caster sugar and lime juice and stir until lightly coated. Reserve.

Place the peaches or nectarines in a large bowl and pour over boiling water to cover. Leave for 30 seconds, then plunge them into cold water and peel off their skins. Cut each one into 8 thick slices, discarding the stone.

Heat a wok, add the oil and swirl it round the wok to coat the sides. Add the fruit and cook for 3–4 minutes, shaking the wok and gently turning the fruit until lightly browned. Spoon the fruit into a warmed serving bowl and clean the wok with absorbent kitchen paper.

Add the butter and sugars to the wok and stir continuously over a very low heat until the sugars have dissolved. Remove from the heat and leave to cool for 2–3 minutes.

Stir the cream and rum into the sugar syrup and return to the heat. Bring to the boil and simmer for 2 minutes, stirring continuously until smooth. Leave for 2–3 minutes to cool slightly, then serve warm with the stir-fried peaches and bananas.

Chocolate & Lemon Grass Mousse

SERVES 2

2 lemon grass stalks, outer
   leaves removed
125 ml/4 fl oz milk
1 sheet gelatine
65 g/2½ oz milk chocolate,

broken into small pieces
1 medium egg yolk
25 g/1 oz caster sugar
85 ml/3 fl oz pint
   double cream

juice of 1 lemon
1–2 tsp caster sugar
lemon zest, to decorate

Use a wooden spoon to bruise the lemon grass, then cut in half. Pour the milk into a large heavy-based saucepan, add the lemon grass and bring to the boil. Remove from the heat, leave to infuse for 1 hour, then strain. Place the gelatine in a shallow dish, pour over cold water to cover and leave for 15 minutes. Squeeze out excess moisture before use.

Place the chocolate in a small bowl set over a saucepan of gently simmering water and leave until melted. Make sure the water does not touch the bowl.

Whisk the egg yolk and sugar together until thick, then whisk in the flavoured milk. Pour into a clean saucepan and cook gently, stirring continuously, until the mixture starts to thicken. Remove from the heat, stir in the melted chocolate and gelatine and leave to cool for a few minutes.

Whisk the double cream until soft peaks form, then stir into the cooled milk mixture to form a mousse. Spoon into individual ramekins or moulds and leave in the refrigerator for 2 hours, or until set.

Just before serving, pour the lemon juice into a small saucepan, bring to the boil, then simmer for 3 minutes, or until reduced. Add the sugar and heat until dissolved, stirring continuously. Serve the mousse drizzled with the lemon sauce and decorated with lemon zest.

Chocolate Creams

SERVES 2

50 g/2 oz plain dark
   chocolate
1 tbsp brandy
2 medium eggs, separated

100 ml/3½ fl oz double cream
1½ tsp caster sugar
grated zest of 1 orange
2 tbsp Cointreau

15 g/½ oz white chocolate
4 physalis/cape
   gooseberries, to decorate

Break the chocolate into small pieces, then place in a heatproof bowl set over a saucepan of gently simmering water. Add the brandy and heat gently, stirring occasionally until the chocolate has melted and is smooth. Remove from the heat and leave to cool slightly, then beat in the egg yolks, 1 at a time, beating well after each addition. Reserve.

Whisk the egg whites until stiff but not dry, then stir 1 tablespoon into the chocolate mixture. Add the remainder and stir in gently. Chill in the refrigerator while preparing the cream.

Whip the cream until just beginning to thicken, then stir in the sugar, orange zest and Cointreau and continue to whisk together until soft peaks form. Spoon the chocolate mousse into the cream mixture and, using a metal spoon, fold the two mixtures together to create a marbled effect. Alternatively, continue folding the two mixtures together until mixed thoroughly. Spoon into two individual glass dishes, cover each dessert with clingfilm and chill in the refrigerator for 2 hours.

Using a potato peeler, shave the white chocolate into curls. Uncover the desserts and scatter over the shavings. Peel the husks back from the physalis berries and pinch together for decoration. Top each dessert with 2 berries and chill in the refrigerator until ready to serve.

Spicy White Chocolate Mousse

SERVES 2 + 2 FOR LATER

4 cardamom pods
85 ml/3 fl oz milk
2 bay leaves

150 g/5 oz white chocolate
200 ml/7 fl oz double cream
2 medium egg whites

1–2 tsp cocoa powder, sifted,
for dusting

Tap the cardamom pods lightly so they split. Remove the seeds, then, using a pestle and mortar, crush lightly. Pour the milk into a small saucepan and add the crushed seeds and the bay leaves. Bring to the boil gently over a medium heat. Remove from the heat, cover and leave in a warm place for at least 30 minutes to infuse.

Break the chocolate into small pieces and place in a heatproof bowl set over a saucepan of gently simmering water. Ensure the water is not touching the base of the bowl. When the chocolate has melted remove the bowl from the heat and stir until smooth.

Whip the cream until it has slightly thickened and holds its shape, but does not form peaks. Reserve. Whisk the egg whites in a clean, grease-free bowl until stiff and standing in soft peaks.

Strain the milk through a sieve into the cooled, melted chocolate and beat until smooth. Spoon the chocolate mixture into the egg whites, then using a large metal spoon, fold gently. Add the whipped cream and fold in gently.

Spoon into four individual small cups. Chill in the refrigerator for 3–4 hours or overnight. Just before serving, dust with a little sifted cocoa powder and then serve.

HELPFUL HINT

Keep for up to 2 days in the refrigerator or open freeze. Once frozen wrap, label and date and keep for up to 1 month.

Zabaglione with Rum-soaked Raisin Compote

SERVES 2

1 tbsp raisins
1 small strip thinly pared
   lemon zest
pinch ground cinnamon

1 tbsp Marsala wine
1 medium egg yolk
1 tbsp caster sugar
3 tbsp dry white wine

3 tbsp double cream,
   lightly whipped
crisp biscuits, to serve

Put the raisins in a small bowl with the lemon zest and ground cinnamon. Pour over the Marsala wine to cover and leave to macerate for at least one hour. When the raisins are plump, lift out of the Marsala wine and reserve the raisins and wine, discarding the pared lemon zest.

In a heatproof bowl, mix together the egg yolk and sugar. Add the white wine and Marsala wine and stir well to combine. Put the bowl over a saucepan of simmering water, ensuring that the bottom of the bowl does not touch the water. Whisk constantly until the mixture doubles in bulk.

Remove from the heat and continue whisking for about 5 minutes until the mixture has cooled slightly. Fold in the raisins and then immediately fold in the whipped cream. Spoon into dessert glasses or goblets and serve with crisp biscuits.

Coconut Sorbet
with Mango Sauce

SERVES 2

1 sheet gelatine
125 g/4 oz caster sugar

300ml/½ pint coconut milk
1 mango, peeled,
    pitted and sliced

1 tbsp icing sugar
grated zest and juice of 1 lime

Set the freezer to rapid-freeze, 2 hours before freezing the sorbet. Place the sheet of gelatine in a shallow dish, pour over cold water to cover and leave for 15 minutes. Squeeze out excess moisture before use.

Meanwhile, place the caster sugar and 150 ml/¼ pint of the coconut milk in a heavy-based saucepan and heat gently, stirring occasionally, until the sugar has dissolved. Remove from the heat.

Add the soaked gelatine to the saucepan and stir gently until dissolved. Stir in remaining coconut milk. Leave until cold.

Pour the gelatine and coconut mixture into a freezeable container and place in the freezer. Leave for at least 1 hour, or until the mixture has started to form ice crystals. Remove and beat with a spoon, then return to the freezer and continue to freeze until the mixture is frozen, beating at least twice more during this time.

Meanwhile, make the sauce. Place the sliced mango, icing sugar and the lime zest and juice in a food processor and blend until smooth. Spoon into a small jug.

Leave the sorbet to soften in the refrigerator for at least 30 minutes before serving. Serve scoops of sorbet on individual plates with a little of the mango sauce poured over. Remember to turn the freezer to normal setting.

Chocolate Fudge Sundae

SERVES 2

**For the chocolate
 fudge sauce:**
75 g/3 oz plain dark chocolate,
 broken into pieces
450 ml/¾ pint double cream
175 g/6 oz golden caster sugar
25 g/1 oz plain flour

pinch salt
15 g/½ oz unsalted butter
1 tsp vanilla extract

For the sundae:
125 g/4 oz raspberries, fresh
 or thawed if frozen

3 scoops vanilla ice cream
3 scoops homemade
 chocolate ice cream
 (*see* page 326)
2 tbsp toasted flaked
 almonds
a few wafers, to serve

To make the chocolate fudge sauce, place the chocolate and cream in a heavy-based saucepan and heat gently until the chocolate has melted into the cream. Stir until smooth. Mix the sugar with the flour and salt, then stir in sufficient chocolate mixture to make a smooth paste.

Gradually blend the remaining melted chocolate mixture into the paste, then pour into a clean saucepan. Cook over a low heat, stirring frequently until smooth and thick. Remove from the heat and add the butter and vanilla extract. Stir until smooth, then cool slightly.

To make the sundae, crush the raspberries lightly with a fork and reserve. Spoon a little of the chocolate sauce into the bottom of 2 sundae glasses. Add a layer of crushed raspberries, then a scoop each of vanilla and chocolate ice cream.

Top each one with a scoop of the vanilla ice cream. Pour over the sauce, sprinkle over the almonds and serve with a wafer.

HELPFUL HINT

Store any remaining sauce in the refrigerator for 1–2 weeks, warming it just before serving. If using homemade ice cream, allow to soften in the refrigerator for at least 30 minutes before using.

Chocolate Pancakes

SERVES 2

For the pancakes:
40 g/1½ oz plain flour
2 tsp cocoa powder
1 tsp caster sugar
¼ tsp freshly grated nutmeg
2 medium eggs
75 ml/3 fl oz milk
40 g/1½ oz unsalted
    butter, melted

For the mango sauce:
1 small ripe mango, peeled
    and diced
50 ml/2 fl oz white wine
1 tbsp, or to taste, golden
    caster sugar
1 tbsp, or to taste, rum

For the filling:
125 g/4 oz plain dark
    chocolate
50 ml/2 fl oz double cream
2 small eggs, separated
15 g/½ oz golden
    caster sugar

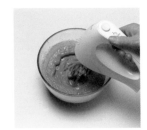

Preheat the oven to 200°C/400°F/Gas Mark 6, 15 minutes before cooking. Sift the flour, cocoa powder, sugar and nutmeg into a bowl and make a well in the centre. Beat the eggs and milk together, then gradually beat into the flour mixture to form a batter. Stir in 15 g/½ oz of the melted butter and leave to stand for 1 hour. Heat an 18 cm/7 inch nonstick frying pan and brush with a little melted butter. Add about 3 tablespoons of the batter and swirl to cover the base of the pan. Cook over a medium heat for 1–2 minutes, flip over and cook for a further 40 seconds. Repeat with the remaining batter. Stack the pancakes, interleaving with greaseproof paper.

To make the sauce, place the mango, white wine and sugar in a saucepan and bring to the boil over a medium heat, then simmer for 2–3 minutes, stirring constantly. When the mixture has thickened, add the rum. Chill in the refrigerator. For the filling, melt the chocolate and cream in a small saucepan over a medium heat. Stir until smooth, then leave to cool. Beat the egg yolks with the caster sugar for 3–5 minutes, or until the mixture is pale and creamy, then beat in the chocolate mixture. Beat the egg whites until stiff, then add a little to the chocolate mixture. Stir in the remainder. Spoon a little of the mixture onto a pancake. Fold in half, then fold in half again, forming a triangle. Repeat with the remaining pancakes. Brush with a little melted butter and bake in the oven for 15–20 minutes or until the filling is set. Serve hot or cold with the mango sauce.

Fruity Chocolate Pudding with Sticky Chocolate Sauce

SERVES 2

50 g/2 oz dark muscovado sugar
1 small orange, peeled and segmented
40 g/1½ oz cranberries, fresh or thawed if frozen
50 g/2 oz soft margarine
1 medium egg

40 g/1½ oz plain flour
¼ tsp baking powder
1 tbsp cocoa powder
chocolate curls, to decorate

For the sticky chocolate sauce:
75 g/3 oz plain dark

chocolate, broken into pieces
25 g/1 oz butter
25 g/1 oz caster sugar
1 tbsp golden syrup
100 ml/3½ fl oz milk

HELPFUL HINT
To make ahead, cook, unmould and store in the refrigerator for up to 1 day, then reheat on High in the microwave. If freezing, thaw in the refrigerator before reheating

Lightly oil two 200 ml/7 fl oz individual pudding basins and sprinkle with a little of the muscovado sugar. Place a few orange segments in each basin followed by a spoonful of the cranberries.

Cream the remaining muscovado sugar with the margarine until light and fluffy, then gradually beat in the egg a little at a time, adding 1 tablespoon of the flour after each addition. Sift the remaining flour, baking powder and cocoa powder together, then stir into the creamed mixture with 1–2 teaspoons of cooled boiled water to give a soft dropping consistency. Spoon the mixture into the basins. Cover each pudding with a double sheet of nonstick baking parchment with a pleat in the centre and secure tightly with string. Cover with a double sheet of kitchen foil with a pleat in the centre to allow for expansion and secure tightly with string. Place in the top of a steamer, set over a saucepan of gently simmering water and steam steadily for 45 minutes, or until firm to the touch. Remember to replenish the water if necessary. Remove the puddings from the steamer and leave to rest for about 5 minutes before running a knife around the edges of the puddings and turning out onto individual plates.

Meanwhile, make the chocolate sauce. Melt the chocolate and butter in a heatproof bowl set over a saucepan of gently simmering water. Add the sugar and golden syrup and stir until dissolved, then stir in the milk and continue to cook, stirring often, until the sauce thickens. Decorate the puddings with a few chocolate curls and serve with the sauce.

Golden Castle Pudding

SERVES 2

50 g/2 oz butter
50 g/2 oz caster sugar
few drops vanilla extract

1 medium egg, beaten
50 g/2 oz self-raising flour
2 tbsp golden syrup

crème fraîche or ready-made
custard, to serve

Preheat the oven to 180°C/350°F/Gas Mark 4. Lightly oil two individual pudding bowls and place a small circle of lightly oiled nonstick baking or greaseproof paper in the base of each one.

Place the butter and caster sugar in a mixing bowl, then beat together until the mixture is pale and creamy. Stir in the vanilla extract and gradually add the beaten egg, a little at a time. Add a tablespoon of flour after each addition of egg and beat well.

When the mixture is smooth, add the remaining flour and fold in gently. Add 1–2 teaspoons water and mix to form a soft mixture that will drop easily off a spoon.

Divide the mixture between each basin allowing enough space for the puddings to rise. Place on a baking sheet and bake in the preheated oven for about 25 minutes until firm and golden brown. Allow the puddings to stand for 5 minutes. Discard the paper circle and turn out on to individual serving plates.

Warm the golden syrup in a small saucepan and pour a little over each pudding. Serve hot with the crème fraîche or custard.

HELPFUL HINT

For a change, make the traditional Castle Pudding by placing a spoonful of jam in the base of each basin. Top with the sponge and bake.

Baked Apple Dumplings

SERVES 2

125 g/4 oz self-raising flour	2 medium cooking apples	custard or vanilla sauce,
pinch salt	2–3 tsp luxury mincemeat	to serve
50 g/2 oz shredded or	1 small egg white, beaten	
vegetable suet	1 tsp caster sugar	

Preheat the oven to 200°C/400°F/Gas Mark 6. Lightly oil a baking tray. Place the flour and salt in a bowl and stir in the suet.

Add just enough water to the mixture to mix to a soft but not sticky dough, using the fingertips. Turn the dough on to a lightly floured board and knead lightly into a ball. Divide the dough in half and roll out each piece into a thin square, large enough to encase the apples.

Peel and core the apples and place 1 apple in the centre of each square of pastry. Fill the centre of the apple with mincemeat, brush the edges of each pastry square with water and draw the corners up to meet over each apple.

Press the edges of the pastry firmly together and decorate with pastry leaves and shapes made from the extra pastry trimmings.

Place the apples on the prepared baking tray, brush with the egg white and sprinkle with the sugar.

Bake in the preheated oven for 30 minutes or until golden and the pastry and apples are cooked. Serve the dumplings hot with the custard or vanilla sauce.

Chocolate Lemon Tartlets

SERVES 2

½ quantity sweet shortcrust
pastry (*see* page 337)
75 ml/3 fl oz double cream
75 g/3 oz plain dark
chocolate, chopped
1 tbsp butter, diced

1 tsp vanilla extract
175 g/6 oz lemon curd
125 ml/4 fl oz prepared
custard sauce
125 ml/4 fl oz single cream
½ tsp almond essence

To decorate:
grated chocolate
toasted flaked almonds

Preheat the oven to 200°C/400°F/Gas Mark 6, 15 minutes before baking. Roll the prepared
pastry out on a lightly floured surface and use to line two 10 cm/4 inch tartlet tins. Place a
small piece of crumpled kitchen foil in each and bake blind in the preheated oven for 12
minutes. Remove from the oven and leave to cool.

Bring the cream to the boil, then remove from the heat and add the chocolate all at once.
Stir until smooth and melted. Beat in the butter and vanilla extract and pour into the tartlets
and leave to cool.

Beat the lemon curd until soft and spoon a thick layer over the chocolate in each tartlet,
spreading gently to the edges. Do not chill in the refrigerator or the chocolate will be too firm.

Place the prepared custard sauce into a large bowl and gradually whisk in the cream and
almond essence until the custard is smooth and runny.

To serve, spoon a little custard onto a plate and place a tartlet in the centre. Sprinkle with
grated chocolate and almonds, then serve.

Raspberry & Almond Tart

CUTS INTO 6–8 SLICES

For the pastry:
125 g/4 oz plain flour
pinch salt
50 g/2 oz butter, cut
    into pieces
25 g/1 oz caster sugar
grated zest of ½ lemon

1 small egg yolk

For the filling:
40 g/1½ oz butter
40 g/1½ oz caster sugar
40 g/1½ oz ground almonds
1 medium egg

2–5 tbsp raspberry jam
1 tbsp slivered or
    flaked almonds
icing sugar for dusting

Preheat oven to 200°C/400°F/Gas Mark 6, 15 minutes before cooking. Blend the flour, salt and butter in a food processor until the mixture resembles breadcrumbs. Add the sugar and lemon zest and blend again for 1 minute. Mix the egg yolk with 1 tablespoon cold water and add to the mixture. Blend until the mixture starts to come together, adding a little more water if necessary, then tip out on to a lightly floured surface. Knead until smooth, wrap in clingfilm and chill in the refrigerator for 30 minutes.

Roll the dough out thinly on a lightly floured surface and use to line a 15 cm/6 inch fluted tart tin. Chill in the refrigerator for 10 minutes. Line the pastry case with greaseproof paper and baking beans. Bake for 10 minutes, then remove the paper and beans and return to the oven for a further 10–12 minutes until cooked. Allow to cool slightly, then reduce the oven temperature to 190°C/375°F/Gas Mark 5.

Blend together the butter, sugar, ground almonds and egg until smooth. Spread the raspberry jam over the base of the pastry, then cover with the almond mixture. Bake for 15 minutes. Remove from the oven and sprinkle with the slivered or flaked almonds and dust generously with icing sugar. Bake for a further 15–20 minutes, until firm and golden brown. Leave to cool, then serve. Store in an airtight tin.

HELPFUL HINT
If the tart is going to be eaten in one sitting, use fresh, or frozen raspberries, squeezing out any excess juice if frozen.

Strawberry Flan

CUTS INTO 6–8 SLICES

For the sweet pastry:
125 g/4 oz plain flour
25 g/1 oz butter
25 g/1 oz white vegetable fat
1 tsp caster sugar
1 small egg yolk, beaten

For the filling:
1 small egg, plus 1 extra
    small egg yolk
25 g/1 oz caster sugar
15 g/½ oz plain flour
150 ml/¼ pint milk

few drops vanilla extract
225 g/8 oz strawberries,
    cleaned and hulled
mint leaves, to decorate

Preheat the oven to 200°C/400°F/Gas Mark 6. Place the flour, butter and vegetable fat in a food processor and blend until the mixture resembles fine breadcrumbs. Stir in the sugar, then with the machine running, add the egg yolk and enough water to make a fairly stiff dough. Knead lightly, cover and chill in the refrigerator for 30 minutes.

Roll out the pastry and use to line a 15 cm/6 inch loose-bottomed flan tin. Place a piece of greaseproof paper in the pastry case and cover with baking beans or rice. Bake in the preheated oven for 15–20 minutes, until just firm. Reserve until cool.

Make the filling by whisking the eggs and sugar together until thick and pale. Gradually stir in the flour and then the milk. Pour into a small saucepan and simmer for 3–4 minutes stirring throughout. Add the vanilla extract to taste, then pour into a bowl and leave to cool. Cover with greaseproof paper to prevent a skin from forming.

When the filling is cold, whisk until smooth then pour on to the cooked flan case. Slice the strawberries and arrange on the top of the filling. Decorate with the mint leaves and serve.

HELPFUL HINT
Store in the refrigerator,
lightly covered, for up
to 2 days.

Frozen Mississippi Mud Pie

For the ginger crumb crust:
24–26 gingernut biscuits,
  roughly crushed
100 g/3½ oz butter, melted
1–2 tbsp sugar, or to taste
½ tsp ground ginger
600 ml/1 pint chocolate

ice cream
600 ml/1 pint coffee-
  flavoured ice cream

For the chocolate topping:
175 g/6 oz plain dark
  chocolate, chopped

50 ml/2 fl oz single cream
1 tbsp golden syrup
1 tsp vanilla extract
50 g/2 oz coarsely grated
  white and milk chocolate

To make the crust, place the biscuits with the melted butter, sugar and ginger in a food processor and blend together. Press into the sides and base of 23 cm/9 inch loose-based flan tin with the back of a spoon and freeze for 30 minutes.

Soften the ice creams at room temperature for about 25 minutes. Spoon the chocolate ice cream into the crumb crust, spreading it evenly over the base, then spoon the coffee ice cream over the chocolate ice cream, mounding it slightly in the centre. Return to the freezer to refreeze the ice cream.

For the topping, heat the dark chocolate with the cream, golden syrup and vanilla extract in a saucepan. Stir until the chocolate has melted and is smooth. Pour into a bowl and chill in the refrigerator, stirring occasionally, until cold but not set.

Spread the cooled chocolate mixture over the top of the frozen pie. Sprinkle with the chocolate and return to the freezer for 1½ hours or until firm.

When frozen, remove from the freezer and cut into portions. Place the portions in a rigid freezer container large enough for them all. Cover with the lid, label and date. Use within 1 month of making. Allow to soften in the refrigerator for 1–1½ hours. Serve at room temperature.

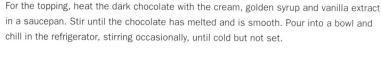

Ricotta Cheesecake with Strawberry Coulis

125 g/4 oz digestive biscuits
100 g/3½ oz candied peel, chopped
65 g/2½ oz butter, melted
150 ml/¼ pint crème fraîche

575 g/4 oz ricotta cheese
100 g/3½ oz caster sugar
1 vanilla pod, seeds only
2 large eggs
225 g/8 oz strawberries

25–50 g/1–2 oz caster sugar, to taste
grated zest and juice of 1 orange

Preheat oven to 170°C/325°F/Gas Mark 3. Line a 20.5 cm/8 inch springform tin with baking parchment. Place the biscuits into a food processor together with the peel. Blend until the biscuits are crushed and the peel is chopped. Add 50 g/2 oz of the melted butter and process until mixed. Tip into the tin and spread evenly over the bottom. Press firmly into place and reserve.

Blend together the crème fraîche, ricotta cheese, sugar, vanilla seeds and eggs in a food processor. With the motor running, add the remaining melted butter and blend for a few seconds. Pour the mixture on to the base. Transfer to the preheated oven and cook for about 1 hour, until set and risen round the edges, but slightly wobbly in the centre. Switch off the oven and allow to cool there. chill in the refrigerator for at least 8 hours, or preferably overnight.

Wash and drain the strawberries. Hull the fruit and remove any soft spots. Put into the food processor along with 25 g/1 oz of the sugar and orange juice and zest. Blend until smooth. Add the remaining sugar to taste. Pass through a sieve to remove seeds and chill in the refrigerator until needed.

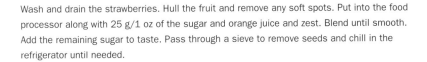

HELPFUL HINT

This will also keep in the refrigerator, lightly covered with clingfilm or kitchen foil, for up to 3 days.

Cut the cheesecake into wedges, spoon over some of the strawberry coulis and serve. Freeze any left over, cut in portions, in a rigid freezer container for up to 1 month. When required, allow to thaw in the refrigerator. The coulis will also freeze well.

Luxury Carrot Cake

CUTS INTO 9–12 SQUARES

300 g/10 oz plain flour
2 tsp baking powder
1 tsp bicarbonate of soda
1 tsp salt
2 tsp ground cinnamon
1 tsp ground ginger
200 g/7 oz dark soft
    brown sugar
100 g/3½ oz caster sugar

4 large eggs, beaten
250 ml/9 fl oz sunflower oil
1 tbsp vanilla extract
4 carrots, peeled and
    shredded (about 450 g/1 lb)
380 g/14 oz can crushed
    pineapple, well drained
125 g/4 oz pecans or
    walnuts, toasted
    and chopped

For the frosting:
175 g/6 oz cream cheese,
    softened
50 g/2 oz butter, softened
1 tsp vanilla extract
225 g/8 oz icing sugar, sifted
1–2 tbsp milk

Preheat the oven to 180°C/350°F/Gas Mark 4 10 minutes before baking. Lightly oil a 33 x 23 cm/ 13 x 9 inch baking tin. Line the base with nonstick baking paper, oil and dust with flour.

Sift the first 6 ingredients into a large bowl and stir in the sugars to blend. Make a well in the centre.

Beat the eggs, oil and vanilla extract together and pour into the well. Using an electric whisk, gradually beat drawing in the flour mixture from the side until a smooth batter forms. Stir in the carrots, crushed pineapple and chopped nuts until blended. Pour into the prepared tin and smooth the surface evenly. Bake in the preheated oven for 50 minutes, or until firm and a skewer inserted into the centre comes out clean. Remove from the oven and leave to cool before removing from the tin and discarding the lining paper.

HELPFUL HINT

Store the finished cake, lightly covered with kitchen foil or clingfilm, for up to 3 days in the refrigerator. If wishing to keep for longer, double wrap in foil, label and date then freeze for up to 3 weeks.

For the frosting, beat the cream cheese, butter and vanilla extract together until smooth, then gradually beat in the icing sugar until the frosting is smooth. Add a little milk, if necessary. Spread the frosting over the top. Refrigerate for about 1 hour to set the frosting, then cut into squares and serve.

Baked Lemon & Sultana Cheesecake

SERVES 2 + 6 PORTIONS FOR FREEZING

275 g/10 oz caster sugar
50 g/2 oz butter
50 g/2 oz self-raising flour
½ level tsp baking powder
5 large eggs
450 g/1 lb cream cheese

40 g/1½ oz plain flour
grated zest of 1 lemon
3 tbsp fresh lemon juice
150 ml/¼ pint crème fraîche
75 g/3 oz sultanas

To decorate:
1 tbsp icing sugar
fresh blackcurrants
   or blueberries
mint leaves

Preheat the oven to 170°C/325°F/Gas Mark 3. Oil a 20.5 cm/8 inch loose-bottomed round cake tin with nonstick baking paper.

Beat 50 g/2 oz of the sugar and the butter together until light and creamy, then stir in the self-raising flour, baking powder and 1 egg.

Mix lightly together until well blended. Spoon into the prepared tin and spread the mixture over the base. Separate the 4 remaining eggs and reserve.

Blend the cheese in a food processor until soft. Gradually add the eggs yolks and sugar and blend until smooth. Turn into a bowl and stir in the rest of the flour, lemon zest and juice. Mix lightly before adding the crème fraîche and sultanas, stirring well.

HELPFUL HINT

Make this when you have a little spare time, then cut into portions and freeze undecorated. Allow separate portions to thaw in the refrigerator for 1 hour. Will keep for up to 1 month.

Whisk the egg whites until stiff, fold into the cheese mixture and pour into the tin. Tap lightly on the surface to remove any air bubbles. Bake in the preheated oven for about 1 hour, or until golden and firm. Cover lightly if browning too much. Switch the oven off and leave in the oven to cool for 2–3 hours.

Remove the cheesecake from the oven and when completely cold remove from the tin. Sprinkle with the icing sugar, decorate with the blackcurrants or blueberries and mint leaves and serve.